STEPPING OUT: RECOVERY WITHOUT AA

STEPPING OUT: RECOVERY WITHOUT AA

A Guide for the Intelligent Drinker

C Shaw

Writers Club Press

San Jose New York Lincoln Shanghai

STEPPING OUT: RECOVERY WITHOUT AA
A Guide for the Intelligent Drinker

Writers Club Press
an imprint of iUniverse.com, Inc.

For information address:
iUniverse.com, Inc.
5220 S 16th, Ste. 200
Lincoln, NE 68512
www.iuniverse.com

ISBN: 0-595-18173-2

Printed in the United States of America

For my mother

Foreword

I used to drink. I no longer do, and haven't for about ten years now. I no longer call myself an alcoholic as well, nor do I place myself in that verbal perpetuity of "in recovery". I belong to no twelve-step group and that, basically, is what this slim volume is all about.

Had you seen my original introduction, you would have been moved by an eloquent vow to avoid bad-mouthing Alcoholics Anonymous. The reasons for that noble intent were nigh-well legion, and not the least of them was a desire on my part to shun what used to be known as 'bad form'. I wanted to come across as indisputably recovered, radically free from support groups, and, God forgive me, *gracious*. But as my thoughts took more definite shape, it became clear to me that I was trying to deal a winning hand all around. Each page I set down, gentlemanly respectful of AA yet at variance with everything about it, gained in dishonesty what it lacked in specific ambition. AA failed for me, as I must assume it did you. I do nobody a favor in the polite pretense that this august body and I can considerately bow to each other's philosophies. We cannot.

Very well. So just what exactly are you holding in your hand? Let me tell you. Something born out of a great deal of anger for an organization that chooses to push to the side its own shortcomings, and which sidesteps issues not in keeping with its own monolithic philosophies; essays that assault the notion of hand-holding and thinly disguised religion as tools for valid growth; more anger directed at any way of thinking that discourages individual reasoning and rejects scrutiny of its own methodology; a plain old arrogant affirming of the power of one person's *intelligence* over endless hours of a perverse group isolation; and, above all, a vehement outcry against the foolish and dangerously prevailing mentality which believes, and would have all of us believe, that Alcoholics Anonymous is the *only way*. It is not.

My aim in writing this is intrinsically contrary, I know. It is an attempt to speak to the ones, like myself, who resist being spoken to. We dislike and mistrust groups of any kind, and we value this mistrust, this skepticism. If this is the reader's state of mind, then he must know that I make no idle show of sharing it. It is and always has been mine as well. Yet I know there were moments during my bad times when one voice would have been welcome. At the right time, and in the right tone.

One image comes to mind as I think of what I'd like to see transpire over the following pages. There were occasions in my past when, sitting at a bar in the late afternoon, I would find myself engaged in a pleasant, short-lived exchange with another patron, begun by nothing more than a shared insight on a wedding party across the street or a fairly esoteric song on the radio. A simple, non-drunk conversation that always seemed more an acknowledgement of two kindred spirits meeting than a wish to discuss the topic at hand. This didn't happen often and would be, as I've said, brief, but it did happen. I have since discovered it can occur over a club soda.

That is why I ask you to read on.

Prologue

It occurs to me that a foreword to so small a volume is a presumptuous thing, although I can't say exactly *why*. Yet we have just passed my foreword. How absurd, then, would a sort of preface be? As absurd, I suppose, as a gargantuan foyer in an old-fashioned cottage.

Be that as it may. What I have to say may not require reams of paper and gallons of ink, but it needs saying. I've given a fairly strong indication above of who I am. I'm not entirely comfortable about commencing, however, without some understanding of who *you* are. Or, better yet, who you are not.

I genuinely hope that you are not currently on the carousel of wretched excess I rode for a number of years. I hope you have not picked this little book up with a palsied hand, and I hope you are not planning to take it home to a) give some false encouragement to people who probably deserve better, or b) delude yourself with a preconceived disappointment following an effort you know you are not prepared to make, or c) to gather ammunition against someone who does not appear to share your boundless regard for Alcoholics Anonymous.

That meager little exercise in humanity done, I can now move on to who I think you *are*.

I think you drink too much, so much so that the alcohol has passed the universal supremacy test and is now an indispensable part of your existence. I am sure that you know this, whether or not you have admitted it to others. And I think that, by and large, you are still, somehow, holding it together. You haven't yet collapsed, certainly not for the last time.

What is paramount to me, however, is *where* you are. I mean that literally. I have taken no note for these essays, nor written and revised one, without a sense of you sitting two rows ahead of me at an AA meeting, a few chairs to the left. You are easy to pick out, because you can't seem to sit still. You are an intelligent person, and scanning the slogans plastered on the walls is not doing much in the way of easing your mind. As the hour passes, the situation becomes increasingly uncomfortable for you, primarily because your conviction that you are no part of the healed or healing souls around you is increasing. As the hour ends, you are barely able to reflect upon what you know to be true: that this AA meeting, like all the others, has done nothing but promote the dreadful sense of helplessness it was meant to ease.

Did you see me, seeing you? That was my last meeting. I do not plan to ever return, myself, although I wish everyone there who *did* benefit from it all the best. It has finally dawned on me that I have no choice but to go my own way in this, and this scares me less than I would have supposed. But, if it's all right, I'd like to take half an hour to speak with you.

And the other guy, way up front, and the girl with the nervous smile on her face.

One:

On Groups

I can't believe I'm taking too giant a leap when I say that you probably care for group situations about as much as I do; which is to say, not at all. For one thing, you're reading this. For another, even those who wind up embracing a group mentality are usually hesitant when they first join. And it is comfortably assumed by most anyone inside (or, for that matter, outside) the group that this initial reluctance to participate is due to a natural shyness. My not-so-apologetic exit from the world of twelve-step, group treatment takes place here. Yes, before I sit down.

I used the phrase 'natural shyness' a moment ago. No problem with the 'natural'; it's the shyness I take issue with.

There is a sort of reflex of reserve triggered in most of us when we're thrown into an assembly of any kind. We get timid, or we automatically fall into our Sunday manners. This is a good thing and, despite the opportunities such a gathering brings to the loudmouth or the bully (a particularly dangerous scenario for a crowd as vulnerable as one composed of alcoholics), it stands as evidence that we are, now and again, civilized. And equally dependable is the relaxing of this reserve, usually not long into the assembly. Some never lose their timidity in a group, but most people can get used to anything, and most can be found sitting pretty much at ease in no time at all.

But an AA meeting is a different animal. It should more readily vanquish reserve from the very start. Much of its strength and a large part of its supposed impact, in fact, depends on just that.

The newcomer to AA is naturally just as likely to feel apprehensive about walking into his first meeting as anyone entering any assembly, yes. The room is filled with fellow drinkers, people at the ready to embrace him and perfectly understanding of the nature of his plight. But that is subordinate to the reserve mentioned above. He is going to a meeting because he needs help, and he needs help from those similarly afflicted. So he sits and in time his social restraint fades, depending upon how quickly he adapts to a crowd. Then the real benefit of the program can begin to work, as sharing commences and true isolation is vanquished. And, again, that all those present are there because of a huge and potent common bond ought to lessen the neophyte's shyness more rapidly than could be expected elsewhere.

A funny thing I've seen in AA halls, however, is that a sizeable percentage of the people present do not relax. Ever. A few of this number are probably in various stages of denial, true, and we can afford to dismiss those we know to be first-timers as well. But there are others, and they are fidgety, and they stay fidgety. Why should this be? What can be at play here in the AA meeting than the normal, transitory hesitancy the newcomer exhibits when placed into a group? Here's a possibility: can it be that he somehow suspects that he is sacrificing something, something hard to define, the moment he sits down?

He is, and it isn't his drinking. He is giving up a small but potentially crucial element of himself: the possibility that, whether for the greater good or no, he may speak in a tone or a voice which will not be admitted to the group, and will not be heard. This is a strong eventuality for any person in any sort of gathering at all, but it takes on enormous import for our man in the AA meeting. The irony is large and tragic; a degree of self disregarded by an average collective is usually a non-traumatic occurrence. Your persona, your individuality, is perfectly safe in a theater or in church or at a political rally, because those kinds of gatherings are not based upon any need to alter you; you already love the theater, worship at the same altar or cheer on the same candidate.

At an AA meeting, however, the sublimation of individuality, necessary to *any* group, is downright dangerous to the individual. That voice not heard is a man's most valuable voice, the one which can be imparted to only a select few in his life. He is giving up a degree of individuality, and the argument that it is a degree of individuality not needed for the purposes of this group is specious and, ultimately, insulting. I believe that an inner awareness of this high cost, and not shyness, not reserve before strangers, is what creates his unease.

Life is replete with ironies, and one I've noticed is that the distrust and anxiety I personally felt about entering a group environment such as AA seems so *common*. Dislike of these groups does what so many programs boast of doing: it cuts through all segments of society. You can see it on the faces of the white collar brokers as they try to settle into their metal chairs, and you see it in the way construction workers shuffle into the AA hall. I think they already know what I jotted down on an index card in a rare moment of clear-headedness. That is, *in getting a group right, you must get everyone in it just a little wrong.* And that *little,* reader—that *little!*

It is the gradations of thought, behavior and character which make us who we are. They are often subtle, and therefore inclined to be lost in an assembly, yet it is in that subtlety that their import lies. What distinguishes each of us from the herd at large may be nearly imperceptible, but is immeasurably valuable as well. And, sadly, very fragile in the midst of a company with a definite agenda, such as AA. Yet another irony: twelve-step groups blast the trumpet of individuality and selfhood as loudly as the best of them. But 'unique' must be, literally, apart. It isn't so much that the group—any group—is intolerant of 'unique'; it's just that no hall is big enough for the two of them.

I've sat in all sorts of groups, especially during the years I was convinced my drinking was merely symptomatic of deeper trouble. It didn't take long before I realized that others present were similarly deluding themselves. Once, that is, I became aware of my own self-deception. But they sincerely thought, as for some time I did, that we were openly searching for answers. And consequently were open in revealing anything and everything to their fellow searchers. In other words, each person painted as *unique* a portrait of himself as could be done.

All of which was swallowed up into the mass of the group, and meant to be digested by and directed to the good of the group. This is, as you know, the guiding principle behind such activity, AA being no exception. What is odd is that I cannot clearly distinguish in my memory which sort of meeting I was attending—AA or more generally therapeutic—based upon the content of what I remember having heard. The more outrageous declarations were by no means restricted to the therapy sessions, and the tales having the least to do with alcoholism were often told within the AA halls. A woman regaling the crowd with her recurring dream of fighting her way through a jungle of banana tress (very true, thank you) did so in an AA hall, while more than a few sharing a doctor's space with me lamented the drinking they had turned to. It seemed that, wherever I turned, there was an enormous range of distressed psyches, all of whom, in telling their stories, set themselves up to be identified with. And it seemed that, irregardless of the meeting's advertised goal, I was never able to shake the feeling that I had less in common with the people there than whatever it was we shared. If that smacks of an elitist attitude to you, I say it cannot be. In asserting my own claim to whatever shades of thought and feeling I know to be absolutely mine, I am just as emphatically reinforcing yours.

I bring up the various kinds of group situations I've experienced to highlight just how limited such a treatment is. I heard everything, and I heard it from every source, motivated by every desire. How is it that I could not rejoice on learning of a soul as tortured as mine, *in an almost identical way,* as, now and again, I did? Because the thing in me, in all of us, that seeks a kindred spirit suffering from a like pain or addiction cannot overshadow the core in me, and in all of us. This core is as vital to our mental or spiritual existence as our hearts are to our physical ones, and cannot allow the notion that anyone is *just like us* to be considered. It is ego in its purest state, and has as much in common with vanity as steel has with cardboard. How tough is it? Well, it's responsible for the recidivism in drinkers whose lives are at stake, who have lost everything and still think they have no great problem. Call it 'denial', but it is in fact the self's inability to believe that it is identical to others. And even the most strident AA enthusiast may not claim to have tamed this inherently untameable essence.

Let's get back to the AA meeting. If I were to try to disregard my individuality for the sake of recovery (assuming such a thing is possible), am I not taking the enormous risk of giving up precisely what would make my being recovered worth striving for? But it is not possible. Not in any lasting way. I give you a day wherein I am feeling unsure about myself and my sobriety. I attend a meeting looking, as so many do, for strength. There is a man there telling his story. He is doing so altruistically, for he appears to be confidently recovered. I listen to him speak and am amazed at how like myself he is. His past, his circumstances, virtually mirror my own. Unfortunately, *what I need* for his presence to be truly beneficial to me is a formula which can calculate all the thousands of conscious and subconscious twists and turns his own psyche took to achieve his state of well-being. Twists and turns, I must add, that my own mind may or may not be able to take. And if there is no such formula, as we know there cannot be, then I am doomed to reappear at meetings on a daily basis because, while there, I am hopeful and strong again.

Which brings us to the need to perpetually attend meetings. On any given day in any given AA hall, the odds are high you'll hear more than one member—with lots of anniversary medals at home—emphasize his need to attend these functions at least once a day. He will often make this statement with a sort of I-dare-you pride. It's as though he's saying that it doesn't work very well, but, well, it works for a while. And isn't that good enough? Maybe the bolstering effects of the meeting only last until the next one, but there are, after all, meetings to be found just about anywhere, and at all times of day.

To which I say, Sorry, but that's not good enough for me. That it *is* for so many is fine; great portions of the population engage in activities in which I want no part, and the world continues to spin nicely. *But I don't want to keep coming back.* And I believe that, the more I subscribe to AA philosophies, the more I guarantee myself a reserved chair in the corner. Group treatments are self-perpetuating because, basically, they have to be. The drinking days, which are meant to be forever abandoned, cannot be removed from the group without also taking away the reason for the group's being there. Coping with the world soberly is the goal, but the true power to do so makes a group support intrinsically redundant.

There is, of course, the avuncular notion among AA proponents that the meetings exist for the drinker on the threshold, the man or woman at the crisis point, who will most benefit from examples of sober longevity. Yet I have observed this to be a fractional part of the system. Meetings are not continually composed of newcomers, all in various stages of recovery, and all making for periodically new groups. By and large, AA has *expanded* its base, and not regenerated it, and regeneration does not occur even in the oldest, most established locations. People move on, not because they feel secure, but because people just plain *move*, and the groups themselves grow to be little more than specific social arenas, with a dedicated membership. And these are the successful ones.

I could go on, but you see my point. As frightened as I was about staying clean, I was more disturbed by the idea that the AA groups would be a fixture in my life. It didn't make sense to me, this group mentality, and it still doesn't. I simply don't understand an organization that fosters dependency among its members yet is downright boastful of its success in equipping them for the real world. There must be another way to get that boulder over the hill, and I can't be satisfied with the Sisyphus-like strategy of pushing it up, only to see it roll back down the way it came.

One last illustration on the subject: learning to live soberly through continued attendance of AA meetings is about as realistic and desirable as testing a new car's performance in the show room.

Two:

A Failure to Connect

There is no group here. This is between you and me, so perhaps I may be forgiven for doing something that I hatefully associate *with* groups, but has, really, nothing to do with them.

I need to tell you something of my history. And I need to be careful, as well. You, my intelligent, dissatisfied reader, can do without anyone's bottle count or list of debts. If you've attended even one AA meeting, you've already heard it all, and I want to believe that you're here because you know that such disclosures are of no help to you.

So what can *I* confess that would be worthwhile? Maybe nothing at all. But my message is one of hope. Not necessarily a shining, pretty hope, but hope nonetheless, and recounting the greatest loss that I live with may reinforce a conviction I want to share: that hope is an extraordinary thing, even in its dullest colors.

That loss of mine, in fact, is hardly likely to create tears or excitement. It was in my mind, in my memory. My memory has always been remarkably fine; I'm the one who can recite the exact dialogue from the obscure scene in the old movie, or recall who was *not* present at a party fifteen years ago. I don't relay this information, as a rule, unless asked. I have more than my share of irritating habits without adding that annoyance to my arsenal. Nor do I think of this storing ability as quite so much a gift or a talent, as I consider it part of the equipment of someone who's afraid to forget anything. Because it just may come in handy. And, yes, it panders to my vanity, as well. I too can amaze my friends. Primarily, though, I believe I tuck little items away because I think they're important. Important to me, at least. And, pointless or not, the power to recall all sorts of situations, historic or personal, remains with me still.

There was another skill I had, however, linked to the memory, which left me one morning at some point in my mid-twenties and the last century's mid-eighties. I mourn its loss to this day.

Those years were, in retrospect, the down side of my last 'up' times. I hadn't been fired from any job yet. My work and my social life were happily intertwined at a popular cafe in my hometown. The mind can of course obscure and glamorize the past quite nicely, even without the aid of liquor, but I think you'd be hard-pressed to find anyone from my crowd at that period who could honestly tell you that we did not have a great time. We worked hard and drank copiously, and were young enough to work hard the next day. The next day always included laughing apologies and hangover complaints. I certainly dispensed my share of the former, but could not be heard indulging in the latter.

For I had added one item to my early morning routine unknown to my buddies: instead of coming to life over two or three cups of coffee every day, I would sip, then down, a large Scotch as well. Throw in five or six cigarettes, and over this breakfast of champions I would daily awaken. And every morning was blessedly the same. Simply, I would wait for the "connection' to take place, wherein random thoughts, moments from movies or past conversations would not just enter my mind, but literally *spark my spirit*. It was not out of the ordinary for me to smile, even laugh, to myself. This happy transformation would happen to me as dependably as the tolling of a highly dependable bell, and I would go into the shower, God forgive me, singing.

(A lot of poetry for what was very likely a kicking in of a prior night's buzz, I suppose. But what drunken high ever felt like just a drunken high?)

As you may have supposed, the current was turned off one morning. It has stayed dead since. It was not a gradual lessening, condensed in my mind over the years to an overnight occurrence; it *was* overnight. The date is lost to me, but I distinctly remember that morning, and how utterly confused I was. Surely, I thought, something is not here that was here yesterday. I waited a while, drank some more, and then went off to the shower feeling…stood up. That 'spark' was an intimate and crucial part of my day, and, while I was not confronted with someone who had suddenly died, I was filled with the dreadful sureness that some*thing* had. And I knew who the villain was. Of course I did.

It's been a good number of years since then, and I stopped feeling abandoned quite a while ago. As time went on, I had many other and more basic survival issues to handle. But I find I still conjure those days. It is peculiar; they are my memories, but they seem to belong to someone else. And I always have the submerged knowledge and more evident regret of having destroyed a natural, human mechanism in myself. I know that in my youth, well before liquor became indistinguishable from everything I did and was, a *willingness* to take on the world was in me, and was triggered by nothing more than a waking state of mind. But I had exploited it; I had gotten it drunk, and was then horrified by its inability to perform. I'm sure a neurologist could tell me, exactly, what I had done to my own mind, and I'm sure the word 'synapses' would crop up. From what I understand, these are connectors in our brains. Some of mine, I believe, got snapped. Or drowned.

I don't blame alcohol so much for this. Not actively, anyway. That is to say, should I find myself in a bitter mood, I've got much else to lay at its doorstep. This loss, so intangible and so intensely felt, happened. It happened, and I think I knew even then that this was the first big ticket I would have to pay in the seductive and grossly unfair deal I had made.

Sort of like any young man's blunder, in which he stupidly gambles away an enormous sum of money. No, not just money. Say, rather, an inheritance, something far from easily replaced.

So deep a lament for something so vague, so seemingly unnecessary to life? Yes. I cannot escape this confession's coming across as a whine for a lost blanket. Yet perhaps you have, or had, a similar comfort or routine in your own life whose absence is in no way minimized by the lack of sympathy it excites in others. We alcoholics are as well notorious crybabies. This is the truth, and not at all surprising. Egocentrism lies at the heart of the most gregarious, open-handed drinker. Therefore, a part of me will always be ready to sing the blues about that particular morning of my life. But, as with the recounting of trivia, I will keep it mostly to myself.

And mornings, these days? Not so bad because, as may be expected, an awful lot of grief has been overcome in the intervening years. I was never truly *carefree*, even in those early days when everything was still functioning. But the gratification you achieve in conquering something rather nasty can nestle inside you and act as an anchor; and, though incapable of replacing spurts of more innocent happiness, can more than adequately keep despair at a distance. That particular safeguard is no small thing. And its existence is the entire point of this particular essay.

Do I call it what transpired in my own past, then, an even trade? No. I'm left with an exceptionally good deal, but it is one that should have never required being struck. I created the loss, the losing situation, and so forfeited the power to bargain and choose. Yet, as I've said, my mornings are all right. On the better ones, I still sing in the shower. Yes, I now clearly hear what I sound like. But I'm strong enough to take it.

Three:

What is Owed

It was not long into my sobriety when I became acquainted with the supposedly indispensable concept of making amends to those I had mistreated in my past, mistreated both materially and otherwise. I did not question this moral instruction. I would guess most anyone, recently emerging from a foggy state and seeing, in the cleaner air, memories unexpectedly shameful due to this new clarity, does not. It draws forth an emotional response from everyone who ever had to face up to anyone and say, I'm sorry. This is admirable conduct, by which we usually foresee a child's impending maturity. Grown-ups 'fess up. And if nineteenth-century literature and its reliance on the power of words like 'honor' touches you to your core as it does mine, then this notion of making good, of paying back, is irrefutable.

So the question becomes why, as I clumsily began plying my steps, did I continually shove this particular one on a back burner? I did not examine it and find it wanting. There didn't seem to be a need to think about it. It appealed to not only what was left of my better instincts, but to my love of orderliness, as well.

Be that as it may. Something was wrong. I wasn't doing it. I hadn't even made a start of making amends; I had no choice, then, but to take a deeper look. See what the hold-up was, as it were. Oddly enough, I gained no ground in this attempt. I fathomed no obstructive mysteries within myself that were preventing my carrying on with the program. There were no mysteries to fathom here. As I recall, it was rather more a case of finally seeing one side of me holding up a placard saying MAKE AMENDS to another side of me, and feeling very distinctly that the placard-wielding persona would have to go. Something like a riot of certainty took place within me. I was suddenly conscious of a simple, appropriate course of action: pay back all moneys owed, and the rest has taken care of itself.

The reader is invited to be as skeptical of that last line as he pleases. Just let him be aware that this is no slick, emotional get-away scheme because, logically, *damage done cannot be undone.* Only some forms of material damage can. And I am getting off of nothing because everything I did, all the abuse I hurled, was *paid for at the time*, and what is left is the emotional residue that stays with us after every experience, that continues to shape us as human beings. Thousands of expressions of contrition, understanding or even gratitude do not remove this. Nor, I think, should they.

By way of illustration, I point to my own history. I look at my past, those parts which were never blocked out and those which have returned to me. For our purposes here, I examine the times I disappointed, disgusted, and generally let folks down. Of course, there were years of functioning quite nicely, of rarely doing a bad job, of remembering everything and never calling in sick. When these misleading days passed and I began losing work, I was always sure of just whose fault it was. It was mine. I may have been drunk, but I wasn't stupid. As might be expected, I would shake my fist and call on the heavens to avenge me on the unfeeling restaurateur who had just discharged me, but that was mostly show. (Mostly. I still harbored, in those days, resentment at not being praised for performing, even while drinking, more professionally than my sober colleagues.) All in all, however, I knew my rage was an act I was putting on for my own gratification.

Now, years have passed. I am clean, and Mr. P comes to mind. Mr. P was a restaurant owner who had fired me many years ago. My dismissal followed his smelling my breath, noticing the inordinate number of trips I took to my locker, and triumphantly putting two and two together. Precisely what I am to do about this man of limited soul, this peripheral figure from my past? I was told by more than one person at more than one AA meeting to present him with an apology. That it didn't matter, that I knew he wouldn't remember. That it didn't matter, my never having stolen from him. Even my nagging sense that making amends to Mr. P would be no more than an exercise in futility for all concerned didn't matter.

To which I say, Those things matter. I simply had to cut through a good deal of my own, and AA's, rubbish to see why.

It took me a while to get beyond my deep-seated aversion to addressing myself to someone who is not expecting to be addressed by me, but it took a bit longer to recognize what is valuable, and essential here, in that natural courtesy. In apologizing to Mr. P, am I not placing before him an emotional burden, *however minor*, he did not ask for? I cannot presuppose that he recalls me or that, if he does, he has any interest whatsoever in what became of me. I am released from any responsibility to account for my past behavior because, in all truth, *there is no obligation to meet*.

However. Let's say that the above, though valid, is quite beside the point. I am to present my remorse to Mr. P regardless of his lack of concern for my welfare, for it is imperative to *my recovery* that I do so. This is the AA agenda. The funny thing is, I've been talking with my recovery, and it's remarkably blasé about the whole thing. We have a future to tackle, it tells me. If I were to apologize, am I not then gesturing pathetically to ease whatever guilt I carry? And that's assuming I carry any at all. Mr. P did what he was supposed to do; he fired an employee who was drinking on the job. I don't hate him for that. However, just as he has no right (and probably very little inclination) to hang on to rancor at having been ill-used by me, he similarly has no claim on the man I am now. All of which, again, takes for granted a curiosity that does not exist. In either direction.

Let the record reflect that Mr. P was, and remains, an appalling man. Had he been kind, I honestly believe my feelings in this matter would be the same. The reasoning holds up; only the motivating feelings change, and such motivations ought not to be trusted when one walks in the terrain of forgiveness. His being less than fine, therefore, changes nothing. He was in my past as I was in his. I acted, he reacted. That is all either of us need know.

One thing more needs to be said, though, before we finish with Mr. P. I hesitate only because it seems too facile, yet I've never heard anyone discussing the process of making amends comment on it.

Alcoholism is universally thought to be a disease, largely chemically based, if not genetically dictated, and has been considered so for some time now. Is it not incumbent on our friend P to understand that those trips I took to my locker were not necessarily of my own choosing? Granted, he would have needed a somewhat finer moral fiber than was in his possession then to have seen this. But attitudes have altered appreciably since even those relatively recent days. If we accept alcoholism as a disease, we are left with the notion of atoning for behavior over which one had marginal control, at best. And that is absurd.

The infamous Mr. P was one of a comparatively small number of employers I…disappointed. He and his fellow victims are, in my mind and conscience, nicely where they belong. I don't think I could have this peace of mind unless I were completely free from debt to these people. I find myself trying to summon accurate phrasing to justify my conviction on this issue, but can come up with little more than an old-fashioned dread of being regarded—by anyone—as a deadbeat. A disease is one thing, but a gentlemen pays his debts. You will recall my using the word 'honor' earlier. It is a vital component of the self-respect you will soon be reclaiming.

Four:

On Those Who Matter

I spend an awful lot of time wondering about issues to which I don't think I'll ever find satisfactory answers. Such as: how is it I am not uncomfortable in generalizing on the subject of, say, former employers, yet am downright wary when we come to the alcoholic's family and friends? I suppose it's just that the latter are so inherently *personal.* Your casual friends could be, conceivably, mine as well. And we may have punched the same timeclock. But your inner circle is yours alone.

We go nowhere, however, without first defining 'friend' to everyone's satisfaction. I face the temptation here to say that you will know your true friends easily, particularly as you battle your addiction, for they are the ones who will stand by you through the worst nights, through the vomiting broken up by insincere promises, and through the foul abuse you shout for no reason whatsoever. That may be a part of the definition, but it is far from being the whole of it. (Horribly, those who *want* you to remain a drinker will stand by you just as staunchly.) It is a mysterious and incalculable business, the making of a true friend. But, mystery notwithstanding, let there be no mistaking one thing: you don't fool anyone if you believe you will go through your life with more than four or five *friends.* Your whole life. You will be fortunate to have that many, and to think otherwise is to walk around with a very poor set of standards indeed.

I knew in my early twenties who my friends were. Since then, a few people have come close to occupying that exalted position in my life, and I have a genuine liking and a real concern for them. But the days when another person could bring to me what I needed to be the man I wished to be are past. (That statement is not so cold and arrogant as you may think; remember, friendship is, has to be, reciprocal.) One of the reasons that each of my few friends stays inside me and colors who I am is their uniqueness. Logically enough, I hurt them in individual ways.

Distance came in handy in my relations with two of them. This appealed to my sense of martyrdom. I loved them, but congratulated myself on having sufficient pride left to hide out, to save them the unpleasantness of seeing the monster I had become. That little perverse glamour belongs in the same playground with my idea that infrequent visits would better enable me to mask my decline. And another friend distanced *herself* from *me*. Slowly. I never asked, but would not have been surprised to learn that this was a sort of social preparation for a complete break.

But there was one friend, an old friend, who had the misfortune to live in the state I ran to, just as my running was at an end. He enjoyed the privilege of a front row seat at my crack-up, and did those things for me that create a divided and tortured mentality in the last friend of the drinker. He didn't walk out of the restaurant when I charitably and pathetically tried to give my salad to a stranger at the next table; he drove me twenty miles to an open liquor store on a Sunday, after I had exhausted every possibility on foot; and he picked up the phone before dawn when I called on the day I checked myself in for the last time.

I recite these things to confirm the depth of his friendship, so that you may know that, despite all of it, he could only get *so close, and no closer.* I say with absolute certainty that, as the drinking progresses, you come nearer to that place where you are inescapably alone with your bottle.

This friend I speak of was no sentimental fool, well-meaning but unintelligent. If concern and/or brains could have allowed an outsider in, he would have gotten in. *That doorway does not exist,* and I stress this so vehemently because many of us, drunk or sober, cling to the notion that one person can make the difference, if the love is there. This is not true. Turn your back on twelve-stepping and revile the world if you must, but do not look for a savior in your own home, or neighborhood. Recovery cannot be achieved save through a frighteningly pure *aloneness.*

You may recall my mentioning insoluble issues I wrestle with. Here's another: why should a verbal listing of emotions, all real, all heartfelt, somehow minimize, rather than enhance, the perceived state of the person who's feeling them? In other words, when I say that my friend was angry at what I was doing, you can see it. But when I say he was angry, hurt, confused and frustrated, each expression of emotion seems to diffuse the impact of the others. In any event. My friend experienced all of these and more on my behalf, yet I was as incapable of empathizing with him as he was of getting through to me. They're both sides of the same wall, the wall you don't even try to break through.

So, one's friends. We have dispensed with the non-important people in the recovered drinker's past, the ones AA would have him seeking out and apologizing to. But what is owed to these people who know you, truly know you, and have been honestly pained at witnessing what you have done to yourself? No more than what they had a right to from the start—yourself. As you were, when those ties which bound you in friendship were first forged. By all means, hate the banality of this, but I defy you, after all is said and done, to call it *easy.* In coming through, you will have earned your continued place in their hearts and lives. Oddly enough, I believe that a great danger for the newly-recovered alcoholic is his potential for entertaining the idea that his friends may not be quite good enough for *him.* While this is psychologically explicable, it makes for lousy company. Try not to lose sight of the fact, dear newly-recovered, that the superman who emerged from the abyss also dug it.

I have not yet drawn a line between family relations and close friendships in the alcoholic's life. If you share my philosophy on friendship itself, we find ourselves with, in fact, only one line to draw. And, like so many landmarks that became evident to me as I spiraled down through my addiction, it's one of the last divisions from ordinary life, from any semblance to independence, that drinking creates in the course of time. (Ironically, as any sickness grows, all non-essential layers of one's life are peeled off. This is no less true for the alcoholic than for the cancer victim. To coin a phrase, alcohol distills.)

That partition between friends and family? Primarily, it's legal. Relatives, as a rule, are expected to pick up the outstanding tabs. Of course, just about all excuse- buying and emotional support will have vanished by the time you get to this point, because you are now near the caveman level. Shelter, the occasional meal and the necessary shower are the things you and your bottle need. Feel free to substitute 'martini pitcher' for 'bottle'. The shelter may be a cot in a cousin's run-down apartment, or it may be very grand indeed. All of that is beside the point. The place remains the same.

But you knew that.

Incidentally: it's no secret that a sizable chunk of the homeless population is made up of alcoholics, but I disagree with the widely-held belief that these drinkers went just a rung or two farther down the ladder than we did. No; I remember seeing the place. Some serious leaping is required to get there. When that last connection to the daily, normal world is severed, when that last hand is slapped away, a chasm is crossed.

I never made that leap myself, though there were times when I would have sworn I had. Why I didn't is dealt with elsewhere. I *returned*, so to speak, and found much of what I'd turned my back on exactly as I had left it. It was no shock to find that those who had known me casually were pleased with my recovery. Mildly, proportionately pleased, which is as it should be. There were no cartwheels and hallelujah cries from those near to me, either. An almost audible sigh of relief was the most I got and that, I assure you, is all you want. The 'making of amends' would in fact have cheapened what transpired. In coming back, you bring to those you care for what you took from them; in coming back, you return to them what was owed.

Five:

On Slogans

An aphorism increasingly difficult to avoid these days runs as follows: Never 'assume', because when you 'assume', you make an 'ass' out of 'u' and 'me'. I remember first hearing it on an episode of the old situation comedy, THE ODD COUPLE. Would that it had stayed there.

How this statement seeped into the public consciousness and gained the status of a truth is a process both disturbing and unclear to me, and one I'll gladly set aside. What concerns me more, and what I must speak to, is how this catchphrase is usually proclaimed after one of its more AA related cousins is heard: namely, the advice to take things 'one day at a time'. The former is intended to substantiate the latter. Which, to my mind, is not unlike claiming that swimming pools are bad news because people have drowned in them.

And which reduces me to spelling something out far beneath myself, presumably beneath you, but, sadly, at eye level with anyone who would subscribe to such nonsense.

Even the most ardent proponent of a one-day-at-a-time attitude must confess that he does not, in actuality, live that way. Every life operates on thousands of assumptions, large and small, made, supposed and fulfilled continually. We cross the street on the very probable supposition that we will make it to the other side. We save money because there is a strong likelihood that we will need it later. And I am most emphatically *not staying sober just for today*, because I don't know what tomorrow may bring. If I am genuinely in doubt about my being around on the next day, why on earth should I not drink this afternoon? This reasoning is unsophisticated, I know, but I can think of no other way of addressing a mentality that seems to believe that the shuffling of a few letters to create other words creates, in turn, a truth. That sort of slogan-making isn't philosophy or psychology, even in their most primitive forms: it's voodoo.

Needless to say, there is a world of difference between ordinary, logical assumptions and the *taking for granted*, the presuming, of conjectural actions and responses of others, emotional and material states which cannot be foreseen, and the like. These are the issues which call upon the facilities of a mature mind, a willingness to look at complexities, and a host of *equally counted upon* abilities adults are supposed to have at their command. Regrettably, they wouldn't fit on a cardboard sign, don't sound cute, and are therefore unacceptable to the world of AA.

There is a mechanism in most of us, I think, which attributes wisdom and power to things writ large on walls. Politicians have never been shy in pushing this juvenile button; all the more reason, then, to resist it. I think of the words that have moved me to learn them by heart; passages from books, quotes from people I admire, etc. How foolish they would appear on a placard, and how well do I know that they touch me, yet leave many others cold. And how like a sheep, or the herd animal of your choosing, did I feel when I sat in an AA meeting surrounded by block-lettered homilies. Never did I try harder to merge myself into a group for my own safety, and find something substantial in all that gibberish; never, *save for the hours when I sat there*, did I actually think of going to a bar.

When you, reader, acknowledge what your intelligence has known from the start, you will never again have that intelligence so assaulted. When you let your reason take the complete command of the situation it must assume; when you let it prevail over all the other aspects of yourself crippled and worthless from drinking; when you trust it to handle everything in your life until your more humane and vulnerable sides may safely reappear, you will know that a place in the herd was never for you, to begin with. You will know each childish, scrawled watchcry for what it is. Useless, and insulting.

Freedom from seeing such things: now, *there's* an incentive for self-reliance.

Six:

A Little Religion

If that somewhat cynical chapter heading has you thinking I'm planning to take on that most Holy of Holies, the 'Higher Power' concept as endorsed by AA, you are correct. I am aware that this is an issue particularly sensitive to AA members, an awareness that has come to me through a series of observations, large and small, at various meetings. I know with equal certainty that, in searching for a common thread of discontent among those for whom the program has failed, you need look no further.

It's understandable that AA proponents should be loathe to defend or explain something so very much at the heart of their agenda, this program that works so well for an untold number of alcoholics, yet is something that sounds disconcertingly like the religious basis for many efforts which have failed. I can appreciate their sensitivity regarding it, and I do not ask that it be made to conform to my own precepts. I simply want nothing to do with it. It is untrustworthy.

Had the 'Higher Power' concept ever struck me as a genuine, feasible *alternative* to finding or acknowledging God, I, and quite a few others, would not be so frequently seen squirming in our chairs. But it has not, because it cannot. No matter when I've listened to the classic rhetoric that, for AA to work for me, all I have to do is recognize a higher power *and not necessarily call it God*, I am left with the feeling that my folks have lied to me. Somebody's telling me I'll understand when I grow up.

There is in fact a paragraph in the Blue Book which I've always been amazed to see virtually spell out this attitude. Almost as smugly as I did. It says, in effect, that those who choose to disbelieve in God, or a higher power, are more than welcome to work the AA steps and that, in time, they'll 'come around'. The wording is as unmistakably clear in intent as it is condescending. (I cannot quote chapter and verse on this: I write without the aid of a Blue Book at my side more, I assure you, for its sake than for mine.)

And that looks to me suspiciously like a chink in the armor. Why feel compelled to refer to a salvation already dismissed as unnecessary? Why tell the atheist, as they do, that he doesn't need to believe, but he'll be much better off if he does? Such argument conjures in my mind the image of a disreputable doctor with a piece of candy in one hand and a rather lengthy syringe in the other.

It seems important that I clarify here something essential to my dispute with this quasi-religious premise of Alcoholics Anonymous: that is, the difference between *genuine belief* and the 'Higher Power' concept as put forth by AA. The former is faith; the other is at best mysticism, at worst, hucksterism. The difference between the two is analogous to suiting up for a mountain climb because you climb mountains, and buying the gear because it looks good. Faith, any faith, is an absolute. AA's theory is an absurd, latter-day attempt to grasp, or instill, it from the outside. Carefully cloaked, mind you, in as non-secular, or *non-religious*, a presentation as can be devised. Not unlike the notion of legislating morality, it falls with a thud.

Do I, personally, believe in God? Yes. So I should have no trouble in following the AA choreography and letting the heathens find their own way. Except I have a problem with any formula prescribed for the masses which fails a not insubstantial minority. I'd be a very poor Christian indeed to allow a discrepancy to pass by simply because I am unaffected by it. Besides, I *might* be agnostic. And Christian, agnostic or atheist, I don't appreciate being told by anyone to stay put, shut up, and wait for the Light.

But let me wear blinders for a moment. I am a Catholic, and let's suppose, not at all unrealistically, that, while I feel for the non-believer, I am just too troubled right now to pay him and his faithless plight serious attention. Sobriety as well as charity begins at home, and I must clean my own house first. According to AA, then, I must admit that I am powerless and surrender to my higher power. Which is God.

Easy? Hardly, because I am left with a precept of my faith which won't go away: God invested power *in me*. He gave me my will and my mind, and the words "Thou *mayest*" ring with awesome responsibility in the ears of the Catholic. And if, congregation of members, you tell me that surrender is still the only way because all my thinking and all my exercises in willful sobriety have failed, I say, with logic by my side and in a stentorian voice, that only means *I haven't been doing it right*. A failed application of what I believe God gave me in no way lessens the value of those gifts.

The woman in charge of the last recovery stalag I visited cut me short the instant I had the bad fortune to use the words 'I thought' in a sentence. Thinking, she informed me, is what got me into trouble in the first place. She then pointed to a poster, horribly etched in my mind forevermore, which read 'Analysis is Paralysis'. Indeed. And this woman may have been the most strident, but she was far from being the only AA advocate to assert this. How many speakers from how many walks of life echoed this in the meetings I attended? I cannot even guess. Each, however, brought to me not hope, but a disquieting vision of some ostensibly benign mobocracy.

The belief in surrender is not unknown to me, nor is it one I disparage blindly. There are sometimes circumstances in anyone's life which somehow seem to call forth this almost instinctive throwing up of one's hands. Situations arise wherein the only foreseeable solutions are more dismal than those situations themselves; we find ourselves in corners, and the way out may cave in the floor. Our heads then act in concert with our sensibilities, and we abandon effort because we are sure that no effort can be made without ruinous cost. And 'surrender' is by no means an exclusive prerogative of the faithful. Atheists let go, too, although perhaps to a destiny less inspiring in confidence. But the mature, *thoughtful* reflex is the same. Your heart and your mind know when to do it.

It is, however, degradingly false and dangerous to give up on the pathways of reason because you are weary and you think they have all been exhausted. To claim that 'thinking' must go because it has not yet ended the addiction is akin to tossing out the baby with the bath water. I believe it is not, in fact, 'thinking' that the AA collective is actually referring to, but rationalizing; the sort of mock-thought that may be called upon to justify lapses in behavior and explain away true answers. Thinking, intrinsically, is guilty of nothing. And we would do well to remember that solutions to complex problems are arrived at, more often than not, after repeated failures.

My quarrel with the 'Higher Power' panacea of AA runs deep, and is, I confess, more bitterly felt by me than most of their other notions with which I disagree. It is, to me, a cheat. In my soul, or as close to that elusive core as I can get, I cannot 'let go' of the sense that, should I attempt to return to God what I have misused, I am doing something foolish. One might even say, sinful.

Seven:

Two Messages

Two messages, prompted by two different but equally valid impulses.

One is natural courtesy; in this case, an adjunct to the chivalry I mentioned in the foreword. I have always found it foolish to discount the importance of social courtesies. It must never be forgotten that they were created and evolved for a *reason*, even if that reason seems obscure to us today. Nonetheless, I was prepared to tuck any pertinent niceties neatly away and get on with my argument. Until, that is, the second force made itself known to me. It is my limited, but kicking, sense of responsibility, and that is somewhat harder to dismiss.

My aversion to the Alcoholics Anonymous way of doing things prompted this small book. I make no apology for that. I resent not so much their having failed for me—the converse, in fact, is frightening— but more, their absolute unwillingness to speak to this failure for myself, and for others equally not at home in their program. I write from experience, and from no short involvement with them; no manner of relating my frustration ever brought forth anything more than an irritatingly monotonous instruction to keep working the steps. From any of the halls I sat in.

All right, then. I wanted, however, to set down no single-minded assault on AA. My intent was to balance my disputes with that crowd with an appeal to the *uncommon intelligence* of the reader, along with my faith in the power of his mind to see him through his addiction. I say to him now that, *if AA works for him*, if it has been the only method of achieving and holding onto sobriety he has known, then he is a fool to consider leaving it. By all means, finish reading what I have to say, if for nothing more than a desire to refute it all. I trust, however, that if AA is keeping you dry when nothing else could, you've been through enough to know just how valuable that is. Idea exchanging may make for a good stirring of the blood, but should not be played with when it's a matter of life and death. And though I want badly to remind him that these pages are all about a way he can navigate by himself, I repeat, and repeat sincerely: if Alcoholics Anonymous has you sober, stay with it.

The second message is mercifully brief. I regret that it must be generalized, because I cannot know at what stage your drinking is in. Ultimately, though, that isn't important. No matter what stretch of the road you are on now, or at what pace you are traveling, it is the same road every single alcoholic has ever been on, and ends in the same place. Accept that as a truth, for it is indisputably one.

Then, understand and accept that, while you are on this road, you are dying. Again, the rate of decline is insignificant. You are dying. And when dying doesn't happen overnight, when there is time for excuses and rationales to create diversions, and when your own mind is being chemically seduced into betraying everything you ever knew to be certain, it is easy, miserably and horribly easy, to forget the most basic thing of all: you don't have to die. Really, you don't. And don't be afraid of living, or afraid of the boredom of living, because *you can live any way you want to.* When you are free again.

Eight:

Two Strategies

One morning in the spring of 1987 I went to see a counselor at my local mental health center. I don't recall exactly what took me there that particular day, but an educated guess, along with less distinct memories, informs me that it was one of several visits paid or phone calls made around that time. A gullible soul might have said that I was reaching out, searching for help, and all in all alerting anyone who would listen that I was in deep trouble.

What I was doing, of course, was covering my tracks. I *was* in deep trouble, to be sure. My drinking had escalated to the point where it was getting harder to rebuild each routine of living—a job, an apartment—upon the destruction of the previous one. This was not, however, the area in which I claimed to be in need of aid. But by pursuing this mental health avenue, I was telling the world that I was making an attempt. And I partially believed it myself.

I brought an old friend to the session that morning. If this was a subconscious device to provide myself with a witness, I was cagier than I thought. I don't believe it was, though. It was worse. I wanted my friend by me because I knew I would need a drink as soon as my hour was up. If I got some sort of miraculous answer to my problems while there, we'd have cause to celebrate; if I was forced to endure more time spent with yet another short-sighted therapist, well, then—why does anybody need a drink, anyway?

I remember standing in the hall of the center, more frustrated by the delay in settling my bill than by a lack of insight on the part of the counselor. Even though I had just revealed, again, my startling perception of my own condition; how I was certain that the liquor was nothing more than symptomatic. The counselor's inability to grasp this was galling enough, but was becoming, as the minutes passed, increasingly less urgent. My friend understood me. Over a few drinks we would shortly come to that wonderful place where, in the same spot and in defiance of the laws of physics, the answer is there and yet no longer matters.

Extraordinary to me now, that I couldn't see why a therapist will have nothing to do with even the most troubled soul while he is still in his addiction. My strategy was chiefly a ruse, I know, but there was a grain of honest intent in it as well. I simply chose to subscribe to an idea or plan so backwards as to be bewildering. I have said that I am an intelligent man and, in a sense, I was acting in an intelligent fashion then. I reckoned that by uncovering and removing whatever psychological stress was at the root of my dilemma, I would be able to *control* my drinking. I would drink like a civilized, sane man because I would *be* a civilized, sane man. Extraordinary, that even a part of me believed such a beautifully comfortable rescue possible.

I felt a shudder in setting that fatuous anecdote down, though not from simple shame. At least, not the shame one might have anticipated. The mortification I speak of here is beyond that endured when reliving a drunken fight, a lost job, or a DUI arrest. It is related more to what you feel when you recall yourself having been sloppily sentimental, when you have behaved in a way that is demeaning to yourself and contradicts your own esteem. Shame experienced over *actions*, however destructive those actions are, is palpable. It can be addressed, even rectified. The other is the humiliation of self-deception, and self-insult. Your behavior may have extended to no one but yourself, but that is more than enough. Trying to fool the world may be pitiable but it is not uncommon, and is all too often seen in sober society. When a person who prides himself on his ability to think deludes himself, however, and wakes to remember it, a wave of nausea can't be far behind.

It isn't so much nausea that follows my other misbegotten approach to a life of safe, happy drinking, but a kind of sadness. And there's no story at all, really. Just a memory of moving, of packing my things as I prepared to share an apartment with an erstwhile friend. I am, as I've said, an orderly man. All clothes were folded, all papers organized, and all bills taken care of before the day of the move. And although it was most definitely not a case of descending order of importance, my last chore was a stocking-up trip to the liquor store. That accomplished, I was ready.

I brought the box of fresh bottles to the house I was leaving that day. Somebody—another friend?— raised an eyebrow upon seeing what I held. I was not affronted, and no bitter argument took place. I said calmly and sincerely that, while I was going to keep it in check, there was absolutely no way I could foresee living without drinking . I was not merely calm, in fact; I was serene. Since drinking was so very essential to me, I would sacrifice over-indulgence for a less jubilant, but at least safer, moderation. This attitude, perhaps the most common, and certainly the most commonly exploded, was both *logical and conceivable* to me. I recall it now and am sad, because I almost wish the horrible truth had come upon me faster. It isn't so much the futility of the drinker's absurd strategies that is painful, as the time that is wasted.

My adventures in and out of bars and bottles mean nothing, narrated as such. You can, as you know, sit for an hour in an AA chair and hear endless variations on the same theme. Many will be more dramatic; the losses related will dwarf my own. But a thousand stories avail you nothing if, at the end, the speaker shyly or proudly demands or begs that you look at him, listen to him, and learn *his lesson*. As speakers usually do. A thousand stories really can't help at all. Not in any substantial way.

Because you cannot and should not let go of just how different, how immune to common experience, you are.

To complicate matters, *I'm* not prepared to let go of how different you are. We are together, I presume, because all the stories told have helped you no more than they did me. So why my own little contributions to the anthology? Because I can only speak to you with the basis of an understanding between us: you *are* different. I write this for, primarily, the intellectual man or woman who has been unable to follow a twelve-step program, yet knows he or she is in trouble. I say again: You are different. I know, because I am too. We are different from the others, not only in that they actually *can* march with the majority, but in that they *want to*, as well.

But we must be even more different. We must know that the ruses and tactics in drinking are shared by everybody, and that we fall for them too. Yet we must look to the deeper pride within us, the one beyond the vanity that, abetted chemically, refuses to place us with the herd. We need to hold onto the pride which acknowledges what the others do not: that *it is ourselves*, and not alcohol, who are fooling us. We cannot give in to the easy and childish notion of personifying a substance. We will not call it evil, or cunning. We need sufficient self-regard to admit to complete culpability, and the strength to summon a greater part of ourselves to defeat a side which has caved in. We need, in no uncertain terms, to save our own lives, and we need to want to do that knowing it will be a duller, more arduous life for some time after the saving.

Nine:

And One Gamble

I'm not entirely ready to quit the subject of self-delusion. It is a wider field than it first appears to be, and I have one more confession regarding my time spent in it. It involves a lie which should not be a lie, a half-truth put forth with desperate honesty, and is a crushing proof of the non-existence of compromise as an option for the alcoholic.

(In sorting this out in my mind, it occurred to me to christen the maneuvering I want to describe as 'dealing'. It fit very nicely, and conveyed the rash, bottom-line aspect of the maneuver itself. Thankfully, I pulled back. That I myself would make a psychological tag out of an ordinary word suddenly struck me as a juvenile and hypocritical thing to do. I resisted so many when in the halls of AA; I'd like to spend my remaining years innocent of adding to that catalogue.)

What happened with me was this: as things got bleak, I made a deal. Not with God, but with life in general. I had stated plainly, almost proudly, that I could imagine no future for myself in which I could not drink. This I recounted in the last essay. What I did see (bravely, I thought) was a perpetual middle-ground. By then, of course, too many people knew I had a problem, and the fullness of their understanding of it varied with the duration of my contact with each. It was to be expected that some would be unwilling to support this choice, and would then be obliged to sever connections with me. My reputation had begun to precede me. My company was still welcome within my circle, but the receptions I would encounter were sometimes guarded. Even the heaviest drinkers among my crowd who, not surprisingly, I found myself with more and more, had developed an awareness that I was changing levels. That I would surpass their intake on a given night was acceptable, but that I had done so before the evening began was placing things in a different light. We were still chums, we still worked together, but something uncomfortable was coming on the horizon. They were beginning to glimpse the day I would have to be discarded, if I did not remove myself first. Or, rather, was *removed,* for everybody knows that alcoholics never politely leave society.

As shadowy as all this was, I don't think it would have entered any-one's mind that I would withdraw myself before the showdown came. And therein lay the deal, the crux of what I had to put on the table. I would leave first. I was already resolved to sacrifice steady employment to continue living as I felt I had to; this would be painful, as I dislike change of any kind, but I would find a way to bring a sufficiently fresh face to the steady stream of employers I would wind my way through. And as for people? My new thinking was that, if push came to shove, I would leave space on that job altar for friendship and respect, as well. No one would mean more to me than my freedom to drink. As a matter of fact, no one did, even as I engaged in these speculations. What's more, I would make the sacrifices I had to make well before the first earnest, well-intentioned talk commenced.

Understand: this was a *completely conscious choice* on my part, as conscious as any decision made when alcohol is in the system. That was, to me, the beauty of the plan. It enabled me to acknowledge my addiction and still maintain it. To this day, the stupidity and audacity of this deal I tried to strike astounds me. But I thought I knew, then, where I was headed. I simply thought that by volunteering for a path most people would reject, I would be allowed to carry on as I was.

I must, however, make it clear that at no point in these self-contained negotiations did I believe for a moment that I was challenging anything other than *the established patterns of living.* The substance so steadily coursing through me wrought many changes and set in motion much personal chaos, but it was always, to me, just that: a substance. It was liquor. It was not a devil holding out a pen and a contract for me to sign, and it was not the God of my faith to whom I was turning my back. The most cynical atheist among us can see that there are balances to be had in ordinary life, that the greater want carries with it the higher price. I simply called out the highest bid at the onset of the auction at which, again, nothing was on the block save preserving the way I then could survive as a drinking man.

For what seemed like an eternity I had, as well, been exercising the routine so many alcoholics are familiar with, and I was getting tired of it. I refer to the combined reality of the drinker with both feet still on the sidewalks of life, wherein he casually takes the drinks that raise no eyebrows and acquires the rest of what he needs on the sly. Setting aside the furtive and paranoiac aspects of such an existence, it is, as you may be able to corroborate, absolutely exhausting. For every hour in the bar or with the bottle I had connived to enjoy, there was another spent in planning the next such occasion the day would permit. It was not long before I resented the shifty little scheming I felt coerced into performing. I do not say that I found it demeaning at the time, because my judgment was so narrowly focused; it *was* demeaning. I'd had enough. It was time to find a way out. I had never heard of anyone actually *willing* to surrender all the normal gratifications I was prepared to give up; to give up, moreover, before the asking was done. I thought I was daring, a dark pioneer.

There is no need here to express the outrage and sense of betrayal I wrestled with as my health and drinking stamina declined. It is easily summarized: I had offered all I had, and I was still dying.

I don't think about all of that much, any more. I have come to understand what my original fear was, the thing that fueled my drinking and grew proportionately with the addiction, and that had me set my ridiculous, melodramatic plans in motion. As fears go, it would be almost comic, had it not been so persistent, so omnipresent at the time: I was afraid of not drinking, because I was afraid of facing the inescapable boredom that drinking first eased for me. I was unconcerned with hidden demons (except as a pretext). That is, I believed I *had* them, but they could be dealt with accordingly without, I was sure, undue trauma. No; it was the tedium of life, of daily, normal life, that scared me. Such a tame beast it sounds and, yes, there were moments when, physically wretched, I begged for the chance to live that monotony. But not for long. Drinking provided me with the means to create my own, ever-shifting reality. I was appalled at the idea of losing that.

It is not my intention here to triumphantly announce that I was wrong, that life held excitement I had missed before and rejoice in experiencing now. It doesn't, but even that will be gone into elsewhere. This story was seen by me, rather, as yet another point on the line I draw out. It is a boldly dark line, and beautiful only abstractly, in that it is purely honest. It is drawn for the alcoholic, and on it is written that there is no excuse whatsoever for what you are doing when you drink, and I mean that in regard to yourself alone. I am as unconcerned with the reactions of your peer group as I presume you are. If you believe you have a reason to drink, understand that it doesn't matter at all. If you believe you have found a way to function acceptably as an alcoholic, well, so did I. It will not last very long, because it cannot. If you are afraid of the emptiness of life as I was, understand that that doesn't matter, either. You will die, or you will stop drinking and face it.

Ten:

Exposure

I have worked over the years in many a job with alcoholics who belong to Alcoholics Anonymous. I don't doubt that you have, as well. Nothing terribly noteworthy there. People are, for good or ill, people, and the sober alcoholic has as few or as many qualities which make his presence tolerable, if not desirable, as the next man.

Actually, the ones I've associated with at the workplace *do* set themselves apart. Invariably, and usually not long after we are first introduced to one another, they inform me that they are members of AA. And if they stopped at that, so too, probably, would this chapter. But they don't, as a rule, and that is what is noteworthy about them.

It is understandable that a human being who suffers from an addiction with so social a taint would be tempted to have it known that he is in the process of being helped. I am obliged to extend this understanding despite the obvious fact that, assuming he remains sober on the job and says nothing about that part of his history at all, I would never have given it a thought. We are confessional creatures, quite apart from religion, and prone to declare that which needs no uttering. And, even though such admissions leave the hearer with nothing to say but an, "Is that right?", I can let it go. If a co-worker tells me he is in AA because he is proud of it, or because he is testing my humanity in his eyes, or because he needs to reaffirm his own recovery status in the telling of it,

I can let it go. All things considered, in fact, I would have left AA alone on this one and gone my merry way. Many of its members don't seem concerned with protecting their own anonymity, but that is little to me.

Except that something more is going on. This particular pendulum of revelation has swung far too wide to be dismissed. I have heard too much; I have listened to too many unsolicited anecdotes set in AA halls, anecdotes which intrinsically involve the stories of other people. I have as well had the anonymity of others shattered for me. That these disclosures have done nothing to color my perceptions of the people so identified is quite beside the point. All of what I write is happening. It may not be happening in droves, but the fact that, in my own life, I can cite more than a few examples is a disturbing thing. Not disturbing because a sacrament of AA is being rampantly violated, but because AA, like many another massive organization, has not adapted to a change in our culture which touches its very roots.

At its inception Alcoholics Anonymous had, I have no doubt, excellent reasons for its strict adherence to protecting the privacy of its members. I would go so far as to say that this may have been its most laudable asset. To the best of my knowledge, no program before had ever fully realized the importance of confidentiality concerning the impact of the stigma of alcoholism in a person's life. The founders of AA saw as well that this confidentiality was essential for the program to work on a widespread, expanding level. That stigma, after all, was no small thing. Anybody with the least amount of knowledge of American society doesn't need a cultural history lesson from me. Although it took a great deal for someone to be branded an alcoholic in the middle decades of this century, it meant even more. It was a scarlet letter of the times, with as much power to socially cripple its victims as Hawthorne's notorious emblem wielded long ago. I suspect that people then felt about as comfortable with the word 'alcoholic' as they do, today, with 'paranoid-schizophrenic'. It carried too heavy a purely *medical*, and thus more frightening, meaning. (And, besides, *everybody* drank. Oddly, the horror of being labeled an alcoholic was directly proportionate to the vast amounts of liquor it was considered acceptable to toss back.) I give AA the credit it deserves for supplying so imperative a guarantee: the assurance of anonymity.

But perhaps you have felt, walking out of an AA meeting, the same peculiar undercurrent I have. You have noticed that the people around you are lingering *outside* with their good-byes and plans for the weekend dance, and that there is something defiant in this. You have perceived that, rather than be abashed, they *want* the world to know what sort of meeting they attend: and that, when they recited the vow to never reveal another's presence in the hall, they are merely mouthing a promise whose need is no longer there.

I don't suggest this to be argumentative: AA and I are more than sufficiently at odds as it is. Based on everything I see around me every day, however, I am baffled by AA's insistence on that second 'A'. The world, most certainly this country, has changed, and changed in a big way. Large corporations quickly and happily point to their willingness to work with alcoholic employees, to help them get sober and keep their jobs. The entire business structure, in fact, has overhauled old attitudes and has shifted to support such efforts: companies receive legal benefits for encouraging treatment for their people, praise for their humanity, and support from accounting specialists who have determined that it is cheaper to fix than to fire. (All of which might be interpreted as a disquieting form of patronizing. But we will leave that alone.) And as for workers not in the corporate loop, those less upwardly-mobile? That is closer to home for me. Yet it has been my experience that the anticipated drawback of an autocratic workplace—a restaurant, say—may serve the alcoholic with equal compassion. In such a case, the owner or manager is as much a part of our society as the human resource director for a major firm. He knows *he* is judged by the judgments he makes and, even in so limited a sphere, he must want to move with the times. Yes, securing your job in a one-owner cafe is more of a gamble, but that's not the point. It's a gamble at IBM, too. The fact remains that assistance and extensions are being made now that would have been unthinkable fifty years ago.

Moving into social arenas, the changes in perception and conduct carry through. Television may be a warped mirror and hardly the best way of examining ourselves, but it is a reflection, nonetheless, and I watch the situation comedies of my childhood with something like amazement today. Not only is virtually everybody downing martinis, the characters with whom we are most intended to empathize are drinking the most. The very long-running BEWITCHED: not only is Darren's new, potential account begging for a drink, we are supposed to laugh because *we'd need one, too.* This archaic attitude toward drinking on television, now so quaintly ridiculous, probably had its last shot with the character of Lou Grant on THE MARY TYLER MOORE SHOW. Television is rarely art, and art may or may not imitate life, but situation comedies desperately try to. It just wasn't doing it any more. Two of the most popular leading characters in t.v. comedy, dating from the eighties? Sam Malone of CHEERS, and MURPHY BROWN. Both in recovery, and both enormously successful with the public.

Lastly, on a practical level, I have found no way in my life to conduct even the most casual of friendships, at work or in a social setting, without the fact that I cannot drink surfacing (which may be imparted, incidentally, with no reference to a group affiliation). People are sometimes overly solicitous in offering a cocktail; people sometimes persistently relate their own excesses in order to get a similar tale from you, or behave in so irritatingly tentative a manner as to make further evasion just not worth the trouble. This being the case, I have seen no alternative but to take advantage of the changes in moral climate we've experienced since Eisenhower was in office. There is scarcely an American closet door that has not opened without revealing at least one skeleton. Adjusting to the lack of shock you receive upon another's learning of your alcoholism may well be the easiest obstacle you will face as a recovered drinker.

These thoughts, incidentally, were prompted by a woman chairing an AA meeting who claimed she ascertained the status of a suspected fellow member by asking, "Are you a friend of Bill Wilson?". I have heard that this is, indeed, a kind of identifying code, used by members in such cases of questionable comradeship. That such a sly, coyly covert question should be asked of anyone struck me immediately as childish and unnecessary. All that's missing is the secret ring and, perhaps, handshake. I cannot believe that a more direct approach would result in a physical brawl or, for that matter, a law suit. (Assuming one feels so strongly the need to trespass on another's privacy to begin with.) Ultimately, the continued 'hide in plain sight' philosophy of Alcoholics Anonymous fuels my cynicism about the organization as a whole.

As for those who go out of their way to let the world in on their secret: the vogue to wear one's addictions and social disorders on one's sleeve is obnoxious but, unfortunately, still with us. I wish I could foresee the date when it will no longer be fashionable to trumpet conditions *sometimes* generated by upbringing. But it must not be forgotten that this immature practice cloaks a decency: a very valuable degree of understanding has seeped into our culture's consciousness. Alcoholism has ceased to be reviled in our minds, and it is unimportant that this understanding may stem from nothing more than the fact that there's nobody out there clean enough to do the reviling. In a world where everybody has confessed to a mask of one kind or another, anonymity is rendered obsolete.

Eleven:

Old Acquaintance

Given my fundamental antipathy to the way Alcoholics Anonymous conducts the business of salvation, the reader will not be taken aback by my fault-finding with another of its steps. The one I focus on here is, granted, one of the program's most seemingly sensible instructions. But I would remind him that anything stemming from an imperfect core is suspect. And, in this instance, completely at odds with a solitary, thinking person's life as a recovered alcoholic.

Newcomers to AA are either advised to sever relations with drinking friends from their past, or are forbidden to proceed with them. Specifically, drinking friends who enjoy their liquor with a gusto which makes them likely AA candidates. The force of the edict seems to depend on who is speaking at that particular meeting: *his* experience, *his* old circle. Should you meet with the same companions and socialize at the same places, they deduce, you place before yourself a massive temptation. And, using the same wait-and-see logic of its religious leanings, Alcoholics Anonymous confidently predicts that you will soon discover how little you have in common with these people from your past.

All right. If a given AA meeting is filled with alcoholics who believe that they can abstain from liquor and still associate with *practicing alcoholics*; if these members would, from the first moment they chose to secure sobriety for themselves, actually *want* to be in such company;

and if they could foresee no problem in such a setting, well, then, fine. By all means, AA must send out this warning. It is, in fact, too mild. AA should, under the circumstances outlined, chain its members to their chairs. For it is only under such circumstances that the admonition to discontinue past relations can be taken with any degree of seriousness at all.

There is only one totally elementary lesson for the alcoholic to learn, or that he may be told, and this isn't it. This is in fact a chunk of what it most assuredly is *not*. I have made it clear that I want to appeal to the intelligent, uncommon drinker, but I can't accept that even the most mindless of the multitude requires such a grossly infantile schooling. I cannot accept that, *simultaneously*, you are in rough enough shape to have sought help and still think hanging out with the guys is all right. Or desirable. Suggesting this as a possible course you may misguidedly take as you embark on your sober path is downright insulting. I fail to see why AA feels it must mandate what must be common sense to the most common of men. If someone is contemplating a get-together with old drinking buddies after the meeting, he never got to that meeting in the first place.

However, we should be done with this. It is after all guilty of no more than stating the obvious. Yes, we *should* be done. But that is not all there is to it, I'm afraid. AA also counsels the alcoholic to disassociate himself from the *people in his life who drink*. I do not know if that is written in the Blue Book, or even sanctioned by whomever makes such decisions for the organization, but that in itself is telling: my understanding of this was born from many meetings in different places, and always from replies to my questions. It is as I've stated it. And I think it is insidious, and dangerous.

I am a man who used to drink, sometimes with friends and co-workers and, more frequently as time passed, alone. I developed for various reasons a hateful addiction to drinking that undermined every aspect of my life. I went into a decline, into a spiral reserved for those with either a genetic and/or psychological predisposition to addiction. Most of the people I used to drink with never remotely reached this state. I stopped what I was doing; they have not. They are the same people they were before, during and after my recovery. Since achieving sobriety, I am, I suppose, different in ways it would be hard to define. Ultimately, however, all the evidence—the ways in which I am responded to, the resuming of natural affections and old ties—confirms that I, too, am the same man I was.

Accurately, if clinically, put. Now, at AA meetings I attended in the first weeks of my recovery, the word was given to abandon those relationships. It was stressed to me that my remaining sober was the paramount consideration. I did not dispute that then, and I do not now. But my recovery was not to take place in an isolation tank. I would have to move in the real world, a world replete with social drinkers. My gut reaction was to defend my old friendships and, in so doing, defend myself. I had a problem: why take away something that was surely worthwhile in my life? Those people from my past meant a great deal to me. I felt strongly that, as long as I took responsibility for myself, there could be no harm in continued contact.

At this juncture, I look for the flaw in that instinctive reaction. There is none to be seen. It is the proper way to view the situation, unless *I am given no credit whatsoever for a corresponding maturity with my sobriety.* And the only justification for that restriction would be to operate on the assumption that I had little, if anything, more in common with my friends than the need to drink. Equally odious is the implication that these people *who know me* would be eager to see me fall, or have no conception of what I've been through. Dear AA, do you think I chose my friends so unwisely when mere drinking companions can be had anywhere?

Moreover, should I discard the people I know, what is left to me? The fellowship of Alcoholics Anonymous. It is offered up to the newcomer as an enticement, as the life to replace the life which must be cast off.

One's new friends are here, it is warmly urged, and they will be better company than any previously known. I wonder. Are there many alcoholics who badly need this comfort? That is, so badly that they lose sight of the natural evolution of friendship itself? Yes, close relations may be forged from one common link, but that is only one of the myriad foundations from which they may grow. And, common bond aside, a friendship will prosper least well when there is an expectation, or even imperative, of such. In other words, the companionship available in the society of Alcoholics Anonymous is as flimsily based as that found in the neighborhood tavern. Yes, the motivations and goals are completely different. Friendship, unfortunately, is unconcerned with the motivating high ideals, or degeneracy, of its participants.

I know a couple, recently married, who live in my home town. I was unable to visit them on my last trip there because both are members of AA and, so I was informed, have taken very much to heart the directive to give up the people of their past. They see no one from the old days, I was told. Now, I would not be so presumptuous as to say that they are depriving themselves of valuable company needlessly, and certainly not in reference to my own. But I did know them, and can't help but speculate on just how much they have, indeed, given up.

Alcoholism is not a thing you do, like murder, that eviscerates all that has gone before it. Nor is it a sudden state overtaking you. It is a *process* and, at its worst, cannot harm what is outside of your own, direct sphere of influence. The changes I made, and faced, after recovering were ample: cutting off my past, removing friends from my life whose crime is the ability to drink moderately, would have served to only heighten the alienation I had to overcome. I am convinced that we who have stopped drinking and have regained our sense of import need desperately to strengthen, and not break, old ties. All that's required is mutual respect, a commodity inherent in true friendship.

To those who would claim that my way of thinking places harsh demands on the newly-recovered, my jaw drops an inch or two. Then I reply, Most definitely. Get used to it. The determination I ask of the alcoholic in resisting liquor when involved with friends who partake should fit, all things considered, near the bottom of that very long list of things he'd rather do without. And I challenge him to name another item on that list with so rich a built-in reward.

In Summary

In which I must address you directly, and use no abstract pronoun.

You are no ordinary alcoholic, for you find it impossible to glean anything worthwhile from a twelve-step program. You resist the steps, partially because you have a skeptical, questioning nature, but also because you know there is something not right in them. You mislike as well the gentle coercion to be embraced by the fold, to cultivate its members as friends, and the tacit implication that your new world will chiefly consist of such inhabitants. Additionally, the inference is there that your old friends will drop away, should you not reject them first. You will hear them referred to as 'Earth People', even as you begin to notice how eager, or at least willing, so many of the people in the hall around you are to accept these changes.

You don't need them. You don't, in fact, need any of it. Understand that people have stopped drinking without such assistance before you, and will in the future. Are they in the minority? Yes. *Just as you are in your dismissal of Alcoholics Anonymous.*

Ending an addiction to alcohol is painful. It is a wretched business, on your own or in a group. And your life will change, because freedom from a chemical dependence will change you. Yet no forthcoming alteration in you can be frightening, once you are free. It cannot kill you. Above all, don't mistake the *difficulty* of recovery for a *challenge so daunting* that it can never be achieved single-handedly.

You possess a mind, the most formidable weapon there is. Alcohol is *not cunning*, because alcohol is not alive. It cannot think. You have that priceless ability, and can reason your way clear. And faith is a marvelous thing, but a turning to faith as the only way diminishes faith itself. And you, and your mind.

Twelve:

On the Road

On the road, taking a route away from Alcoholics Anonymous. We will, however, pass them on the way back.

Not very long ago, a policeman stopping you for driving under the influence was an embarrassing situation, a nuisance, but little more than that. The man or woman under suspicion could choose from an array including, but not limited to, clout, charm, respect, pity and contrition to avoid receiving the dreaded ticket. These ploys worked more often than not and it is interesting that, in some cases, they are still allowed to work today. (This may say something about how reluctant members of our police may be to relinquish their personal veto, but I'd rather leave that be.)

Such get-aways are rare these days, of course; times have changed. The drunk driver is going to be *punished*, and he knows it. He would be overjoyed to learn that a ticket was the only thing coming his way. But he now knows, through the history of a friend or an acquaintance, the circus that awaits him in the year following his arrest. He doesn't know all the details, for they are many and hard to recall, but he knows he is in for it. He is, indeed. Based upon my own experiences after a DUI arrest, I am compelled to say that the penalties involved are nothing short of ridiculous.

Our hypothetical drunk driver should be thrown into jail, and not just overnight. As I should have been.

My own arrest and the subsequent year of hoop-jumping, probationary chores I did were in no way helpful to me. Quite the contrary. Practically all of it was insufferable. I write this because the matter of drunk driving *cannot be dismissed* because efforts are being made to curtail and/or punish it. Because the efforts are are not merely insufferable; they are sloppy. We cannot accept that more stringent measures are being taken and let it go at that because these measures are ineffectual and, in some instances, nonsensical. The thought of spending time in jail is so painful as to be incomprehensible to me, yet even now, years after the fact, I wonder if I would not have preferred this alternative to the inconvenient, glorified scoldings I endured. I know I considered it then. And all my theorizing isn't even taking into account what I *deserved.*

This country doesn't quite know what to do with drunk drivers. Still. The last twenty years have seen massive changes, yes, and I'm told that Mothers Against Drunk Driving is a more powerful lobbying force than the ostensibly ducal NRA. That is not surprising. What *is* unexpected is just how minimal, in fact, those changes have been. All the MADD outrage, all of its irrefutably justified fury, has accomplished no more than taking the punishment for drunk driving to the most extreme state hand-slapping can reach.

Why this bizarre leniency? Because drunks aren't criminals. Not really. Well, they *are,* but only behind the wheel. Most of the time, a great many are good citizens, with as little intent to do harm as the rest of us. It is not coincidental that it is *mothers* against drunk driving; the corrections assigned to the offenders are reminiscent of a stereotypical mother's chastising of an unruly teen. They are instructional and they curtail freedoms; just as a parent would order a child 'grounded'. They are meant to give the guilty party much to think about. And they are cumulative, as well. It is assumed that, the more is piled on, the greater will be the lesson learned.

I never actually thought about prison as a possibly preferable alternative to probation until I was about half-way through my own. Have you served it, reader? If it is over, can you now objectively look back and recall the frustration you felt, and the impatience you heard in the mutterings of your fellow offenders? I can. (But please remember, before I go on, that it was not my *offense* I thought debatable; only the juvenile way it was addressed.)

I knew I was in for some serious nonsense when, the day after my arrest, I was given a permit for the following ten days. Two officers were unable to explain the reasoning behind this gift to me. Another informed me that it is meant in a compensatory way. I had ten days to drive to the places I needed to go, in order to work out how I would be able to get to them in the months to come. Including the driving school, which is usually situated on the outskirts of town. I rejected that answer as absurd five minutes after I heard it. Putting aside the meager courtesy of facilitating my future travel arrangements, there is nothing there but a slap to the public's face. I was arrested while driving drunk. By what rationale should I, or anyone so convicted, be granted the power to do it again? That is to say, given the severe possibilities of what damage I may have caused earlier, possibilities responsible for the creation and carrying out of all DUI measures, I most certainly should have to re-earn my privilege. From the very beginning. The ten-day pass is tantamount to a temporary gasoline credit for pyromaniacs.

We move on, to the driving school. If education and correction are the goals, I beg the courts to find a suitable disguise and chat with the DUI offenders on their cigarette breaks between videos. They may find a cause for the recidivism that puzzles so many members of MADD. From what I observed, any sense of remorse was completely eclipsed in the minds of these people by their feeling of being unnecessarily *scolded*. The over-all atmosphere is uncannily similar to that found in a high school detention hall. The people in my driving school class were resentful to the extent that they believed they had nothing to learn there. I remember this small collective. Four of them left still convinced that a person can effectively sweat out the alcohol in his system. The brightest gentleman was sanguine about the whole affair; it was silly, but not as bad as his last one (he was on his fourth). Most prevalent of all was that ambiance of unfairness in the air, mingled with good old-fashioned denial. Every outdoor conversation commented on it, and camaraderie was achieved through the relaying of useful tips on the best and easiest ways to put in community service hours.

Then we have the mandatory Victim Impact Panel, a ghoulish enterprise conceived, no doubt, as strong medicine for so serious an illness. In this three hour travesty, wherein genuine pain is paraded before an indifferent assembly, actual victims of DUI accidents and/or their relations tell their stories. The results of mine were dismal, and I was paying very close attention to the speakers *and* the hundreds of offenders in the hall. The anguish of the people who had suffered, who had lost children or spouses to drunk driving, was real. So was the blanket of apathy in the room. All the offenders, all those who might well have been the inadvertent murderer of the child the father on stage was speaking of, yawned, shifted, and checked their watches. I believe, however, that what I saw has less to do with the cold-bloodedness of the human animal than with a diabolical combination of: the massive inundation of horror as presented on the evening news; the sad fact that sincere grief does not, as a rule, carry to crowds; and the *absolute refusal* of the offender to conceive of himself as being capable of such an offense. This is a disturbing variation on denial. He can concede that this might be the case, *but only if he were as bad, as stupid a drinker, as the actual driver involved.* Which he is not, or most definitely never will be again.

There is more in this carnival of probation. Community service, for example. It is a fine notion, but it is acceptable only if there is no concern for the welfare of the offender. There is here, as elsewhere, no one to see if any morality is getting through. The community may see fewer tin cans on its streets or the library may boast sequentially correct books, but at no stage of the game is the person on probation tested as to the development of finer social awareness. Is that fair? Perhaps. But only, then, as a partial measure, as a punishment, and not a corrective. Then there are the not insubstantial sums of money which must be paid to the probation board. It would be nice to think that it is used for all kinds of civic good, but I can't quite shake the feeling that it simply feeds the beast itself. Which, again, would be all right, if the beast worked. Additionally, we are faced with educational counseling. That translates to classes which are an extension of the driving school's program, or a personal counseling option. I chose the latter. It cost more, but was the only thing I felt to be of value from the entire ordeal. It was recommended to me by that sanguine gentleman from the school. The counselors don't care, he told me; you can talk about football, if you like.

And, throughout it all, AA meetings are compulsory. The required count is high, in the beginning: something like one per day, for the first month. Then they taper off, as the dosage of a prescribed medicine is diminished. It is ridiculous. As I set out in this small book to speak to alcoholics disenchanted with AA, this particular segment, the drinkers who believe they are there only because they were unlucky that night, was not in my thoughts. Oh, yes, they are unhappy, and they deserve some sort of consideration, but it may not be found here. Nor is it in an AA meeting. In a sweeping generalization for which I do not apologize, they belong in a bar. With no car keys on them.

I had asked the probation board if there were no alternatives to the AA meetings. I said I understood that they needed evidence of treatment, but that, since a set of scrawled initials was all they demanded as proof of AA attendance, might I not volunteer to have my blood tested? I would have been equally happy to have them connect with the counselor I was seeing. In other words, I was so serious about my recovery that I did not want to jeopardize it with further meetings, and I conveyed this, as I say, *open to an alternative of their choosing.* There were no alternatives. It does not lessen my distaste for Alcoholics Anonymous that it is the chosen panacea of local government; nor does such a mindless distribution of addicted people enhance my regard for the powers that be.

To all legislators, victims and relatives of victims: your strategy, as is, fails. You admit this yourselves. I believe you have the right to imprison anyone driving in an impaired state. Do not worry about the stigma of jailing a non-criminal; as this is enforced, the *stigma will change.* Act on this premise, and work out a humane time frame for the offender. You may even curb the number of culprits on their third or fourth go-round. You may not. But you will no longer be guilty of evasion, of tossing thousands of alcoholics against a wall in the hope that they stick.

Afterthought

I watch the news now and again, and feel blessed indeed that I am not among the learned and select few who draw up, ratify and amend the laws of this country. Our legal system is a fascinating apparatus, and I'm awfully glad I'm not there when a debated issue must be interpreted, or be made, into law. Right or wrong has unexpected and complicated shadings; intent or the lack thereof is a hornets' nest, whatever the crime or subject.

This sense of being fortunate I carry is multiplied immeasurably when we talk about harming someone while driving drunk. I was on the road quite often after drinking. (Technically, *anything* I did was after drinking.) I can distinctly recall deliberately weaving between three lanes one night, hoping that I would be stopped. Even knowing that it would mean an arrest. I wasn't stopped, and I made it home that night. And no, I never hit anyone.

The law, however, does not concern me when I think about nightmares I myself escaped. Let the legal and punitive repercussions of injuring or killing someone while impaired appropriately address drunk driving and punish drunk drivers. Let them do so severely, as severe is the recklessness of the crime.

But the specter of the possibility of my having harmed or killed someone haunts me, even today. It comes to me as do mercifully brief nightmares of drinking again. It haunts me because I really *should have,* given the odds. And it haunts me because I honestly can think of no way to reconcile such a calamity with a life of sobriety. I can't imagine carrying on a remotely normal life with such an act behind me. This failure to foretell even an unlikely path to some kind of self-absolution, or peace, frightens me. I don't have all the answers by any means, but I'm usually confident that they are somewhere there to be had. In this instance, I have no such anchor.

Perhaps I need to take my own advice, and consider this more thoughtfully. Learning to live with the abhorrence of having hurt someone in the most stupid and needless of ways? Maybe a new state of mind, a different kind of maturity, would come into being. I will think about this from time to time, because I have no choice. But I will always be thankful that I deal with it hypothetically.

Thirteen:

Periods of Adjustment

There are not many situations in life quite as all-around exasperating as that of finding yourself to be the odd man out. I do not refer to the uninvited guest syndrome so much, as I do that uncomfortable sense of not fitting in when you are precisely where you are supposed to be. You were *meant* to attend the party; you may, in fact, be the guest of honor. But it all feels wrong, because you feel somehow counterfeit. And the longer the situation continues, the more unreal does it become. An existential quality makes itself known to you, for you have nowhere to turn but to yourself.

A correct, if almost too poetical, description of how I felt during my tenure with Alcoholics Anonymous. Particularly in the beginning, before my own thoughts took definite shape. I do not speak here of the more philosophical differences I uncovered between myself and that redoubtable body, most of which litter these pages. Rather, I'm addressing something of a more personal nature, something perceived as a sensation and not a thought. It basically comes down to what I was seeing or, more precisely, what was resolutely being shown to me in the rooms of AA. Frankly, at virtually every meeting I attended, there seemed to be a riot of resumed and recaptured *feelings* going on. And I was completely in the dark.

I do not normally view myself in an outcast role. When life presents events which do not automatically embrace me, I accept it, knowing of the balances to be found elsewhere. And I tend to absent myself from anything most likely to take place in a setting where extra chairs must be brought out, anyway. So I don't believe I speak from any insecurity, any resentment at *not* blending in. Yet, with AA, I could not lose the suspicion that what was going on around me was a sort of benign conspiracy. At just about every meeting, someone would rise to share his history and would, in no time at all, lament the hardships he was facing in being sober in a sober world. Then, unfailingly, he would delve into the enormous range of *feelings* with which he was just beginning to wrestle. He would talk about facing these *feelings* without the numbing effect of alcohol, and the fear this generated in him. In his life now, anger had to be confronted as well as euphoria. There was no telling which *feeling* would next overtake him, and all of it was strange, and all of it was thrilling. He would finish his tale, and confirmation after confirmation would follow. A festival of people with this new-found, wondrous dilemma in common.

They may as well have been talking about the joys and terrors of flying to another planet, to me. They all would speak of what sounded like a difficult, but highly rewarding, challenge. Unexpected (because, you see, they'd forgotten the feelings they had known), but, above all, *interesting*. Where then, were mine? The stories all indicated that this resurgence of selfhood has to be faced as soon as your body and brain are free of the poison of liquor. My system was cleansed, but there was no elation. All the emotions we cherish were conspicuously missing. And I would have sold a large chunk of my soul to have taken on the anger alone.

For, since the very beginning of my recovery, I felt little, if anything, about anything at all. As extreme as that may sound, it is not, I assure you, overstated here. Instead of *feelings* (which, continually italicized, take on a sarcasm I like), I came across what can only be described as an expanse of boredom. With nothing visible on the horizon. Every single activity, even those that had given me pleasure before liquor had become my ruling passion, was mundane, something to be endured. I did have the renewed physical stamina of a system rid of a certain drug, but that is a different thing; it brought with it, unfortunately, no emotional equivalent. As frightful as it may come across to the uninitiated, I distinctly thought more than a few times that, unless I were much mistaken, this emptiness was what got me immersed in liquor in the first place.

It is ironic and almost funny that the only *feeling* I began to sense welling up in me was another kind of anger, born out of impatience. Impatience that stemmed from the jolly or distraught, calm or fearful, but always gloriously sensate, person at my local AA hall, and his story. His story, no matter who he was each time, took for granted that what he was going through was an experience inevitable to all in recovery. And, honestly, many heads were nodding and many chuckles were heard, all in perfect empathy with the speaker. I would chuckle too, going along with the prevalent mood of the crowd. I was new to this world, and my recovery was limited, then, to having survived yet another ghastly withdrawal. I simply thought something was wrong with me.

Only later did I come to see that many of the empathatic responses I saw and heard from the AA crowds were not fully genuine, that those nodding in accord with the speaker's enthusiasm were trying painfully hard to believe he was speaking for them.

Time passed at a pitifully slow rate in those days, but it did pass, and I reconciled my growing distaste for AA (inseparable from my incomprehension of the purpose of the 'steps' and the dawning conviction that I was unlike the people there) with the first efforts to think my way through that I would make. This void within me, this awful dullness, could not go on. I thought about my past, and there were no mysteries lurking there. In the earlier days, drinking had supplied what I felt to be missing, or inactivated, in me. Later on, drinking and coping with the onslaught of trouble I had created while drinking were more than sufficient to keep me occupied. But I couldn't drink anymore. If I did, I would die. And I was not prepared to die yet. Certainly not in so painful a way, and certainly not before I had exhausted every means to finding what it was I'd been missing, *or incorrectly approaching*, all along. I needed a new *modus vivendi* for myself, and that I would have to discover it removed from the grinning, complacent ranks of AA was, perhaps, the first relief I knew.

So I would think and, while I thought, I waited. Perhaps a natural reawakening of emotion, any emotion, would occur. I know that I was not anticipating a miraculous light to flare or a command performance from a heavenly choir, but something gradual, at least, had to be coming my way. Confident that no human being ever carried on for too long in such a state of ceaseless ennui, I did the things I was supposed to do. Many of them are outlined in a previous essay, and that those specific activities were not conducive to welcome emotion is an understatement. I looked for work, couldn't find any, and so cleaned other people's homes until more dependable employment could be had. I'd walk home from an apartment I had just scoured and consciously explore my own state of mind. Metaphorically speaking, I stuck pins in my soul. Could I feel anything? Not yet. I sorted out library shelves for the good of a community irritatingly interested in shifting, and not reading, the books held there. I spent Monday nights watching videos of bodies mangled in DUI accidents. Nothing. I logged in my AA meeting time with my probation officer. I attended those meetings, nursing my animosity to the organization as a parent will care for an only child too solicitously, because it is all he has. A sense of *relief* was discernible in me, as the months went by and I could see how the probationary chores were lessened with each that passed. But that didn't really count. Relief is a reactive emotion and, desperate as I was to mark something positive in my ledger, I was mindful of its impending departure with the last of those monthly visits. Thus, all that time dragged on with no light, and no real feeling. No, so to speak, nothing.

But that was years ago and, while I am usually loathe to admit it when anything slips by me, I do so now with pleasure. The reality is that *something had to have been happening*, happening within me and without my conscious knowledge. Slowly happening, so slowly as to be imperceptible. I must logically assume, based on what I know was true then and what I am sure of know, that a change took place within my spirit. It occurred at roughly the pace, and in the manner, of a city skyscraper's uprising; it never appears to be close to completion until it's occupied. I didn't awake one morning with a joyful noise. That would have been nice, as the peculiar shutdown of certain emotional pathways I related earlier *was* just so abrupt. However, that hated trudging along I had done over the prior year, the meeting of the obligations, had supplied something essential to my nature. As each task was completed, as I drew nearer to independence, I approached a state of *personal freedom*. Freedom. How much is expressed in that one word, so much so that it can gain no more in any further expression? I'm convinced that this is the *most important and last to be recognized* possession we throw away when we discard our sobriety. More crucial than friendship or love, for they can exist only as states of indebtedness, emotional or otherwise, where there is no freedom.

What feelings do I sustain now? I am bound by my own discourse to reveal this, yet I hesitate. I hesitate in part because I am stubborn and do not like to admit to feeling, no matter how indispensable to a human I know it to be. I simply fear being associated with an *excess* of feeling. This is an impractical attitude, I know, especially since witnesses can be found to readily testify that I do indeed over-react, fly off the handle, and generally do all those things I think of as vulgar. I suffer from desiring an old-fashioned image for myself I continually fail to maintain.

Be that as it may. Happily, I can swear to possessing a full emotional life without sacrificing my dignity, because it all comes down to logic. A rather beautiful logic, in fact. The truth is that, as my appreciation of the self-dependency I spoke of increased, feelings were…allowed. By me. There is nothing cryptic here; it is, as I say, almost mathematical. It would be impossible to calculate how many personal inclinations and dislikes I sacrificed as my addiction took hold, and when. But all those sacrifices were made, given without thought, given with an eye always on the next bottle and with no consideration of the loss. With awareness of my own self-control, however, comes the power of choice-making, which, in turn, permits choices themselves to be considered. In doing so, I must reflect on my likes and dislikes, on what I prefer to what is disagreeable. And in this process my feelings manifest themselves. Again. They are given space to emerge, because I *need* them again.

This knowledge of absolute self-sufficiency has, I believe, finally fully dawned on me. It has taken years. Well, so be it. Time itself is as eroding or constructing a force as what takes place within it. There can be no doubt that, as the length of your own sobriety stretches, the emotional potentials before you will be magnified.

Allow me to say again that I do not overflow with joy. I try not to overflow at all. I mentioned before, however, how a sense of self-reliance, of knowing that you will no longer hurt yourself, can act as an anchor within you. That is my meaning here. Nothing can ever harm me as I so painstakingly harmed myself. I am independent of that misery and thus assured of my liberty in the ways of the world, with all the advantages a free man may enjoy.

No, nothing is the same as I remember it from my youth. What of it? Those who have never touched a drink in their lives will tell you that pleasures often are less intensely felt as time passes. Yet few are as appreciative of what remains to be had in life than those who have escaped a premature doom, and see the world in a different light. Light is a wonderfully useful metaphor. I know of no better illustration of the subtle, yet potent, mutation of a point of view than George

Eliot's, in MIDDLEMARCH: "...But whatever else remained the same, the light had changed, and you cannot find the pearly dawn at noonday."

Fourteen:

Taking Stock

It was never my desire to vivisect the twelve steps in the Alcoholics Anonymous program, one by one. Oh, it can be done, and with ease. Much of their vulnerability lies in their greatest strengths, in their appeal to a commonality; the quasi-religious tone, the marching band forthrightness. Above all, there is an appalling elementary school primer style to them which practically cries out for criticism, if not ridicule. But I am also aware that few edicts so ingrained in the public consciousness are immune to scrutiny. I know too that an attack of any popular cultural tradition may generate interest where none is deserved, and attract attention through the shameful device of pandering to iconoclastic or adolescent minds.

I have examined and dismissed as poorly conceived a few of AA's steps because I had to. I had to examine them very carefully some time ago, or I would have been left with abandoning a course of recovery for no real reason other than my antipathy to group situations. I had to be sure my antagonism was coming from my reasoning, and not my aversion to crowds; that my *mind* was as offended as my sensibilities were. It was, and my hope is that my reasoning translates at least coherently on paper.

Which brings me to the last step I want to discuss. Inventory. The step in which you are, on a daily basis, to record the less tangible activities of your day. It is intended to be a way of keeping tabs on the kindnesses you performed and the wrongs done, by word or by deed, to people you encounter throughout that day. No incident is too trivial for this journal; newcomers are advised to set it all down, for all that transpires between you and the world is a barometer of the sort of person you are learning to be. And it is thought that, through perseverance and study of this on-going process, you will be better able to *shape* the man or woman you wish to be.

If this sounds at all familiar in a vague way, it is. If you yourself did not make such lists while in your teens, someone in your circle did. More on that in a moment.

A mental examination of one's own behavior, conducted in the solitude of the evening, is a praiseworthy thing. It demonstrates a consciousness of the impact every one of us has on our surroundings. And this is of course hardly a new pastime. Rational people have looked over their days, admitted their small crimes, and congratulated themselves on little actions performed above and beyond what was expected since rational people first walked the earth. Some do it through prayer; one must recount sins before they can be forgiven. Others tally the pluses and minuses of their roles in that day's rotation while doing the dishes. In one form or another, I imagine this pursuit is inherent in the intelligent human being: reflective, in the truest sense of the word.

AA, however, is not content to let this soul-searching business remain in one's head. They insist that it all be *written down,* and are implacable in this detail. And that, I'm afraid, turns a potentially noble, private avocation into something sophomorically ambitious. I mean that quite literally; it is similar to the list-making of a teenager mentioned a moment ago, a teenager determined to upgrade himself. No, there's nothing terribly wrong in that, even if we could track just how sadly ineffectual such practices are. (Can *any* teenage resolution survive graduation day? I doubt it.) Nonetheless, it may be a useful strategy for an adolescent. It may help him to put things in perspective, a desperate need in those years, and, again, there is something admirable in his *try-ing to instill valuable practices* in his developing character, while it is just so formative. But that youthful age is pivotal, here. Only in those years may such a prosaic application be undertaken with any hope of success; the rest of us are doomed to *repeat* our past follies of behavior, or summon *again* our better natures. Both of which occur despite or because of our best intentions, and without a notebook. Unless, reader, you are currently in your freshman year, maintaining and perusing a personal log will serve little actual purpose towards a goal of self-improvement. I suggest knitting while you ruminate on your day, or building a model aircraft. You may or may not receive insight on your own betterment as a person, but you're assured of *something.*

Why carp over something so apparently trivial? Because it is yet another AA instruction which exists only to support itself, and *will not take intelligence into consideration.* It presumes that you will not take daily account of your actions unless you are compelled to do so. This is nonsense. If I must spell out on paper something beneficial I have done to another that day, as well as every stupid or harmful word I said or move I made, than my problems run much deeper than alcoholism. And if *that* is the presumption, than I am in the worst place possible to find the individual help I sorely need. Obviously, I am unable to confront myself honestly, in the smallest of affairs. Which brings us around full circle: how did I ever know I needed help, to begin with?

Juvenile enterprise aside, list-making can be an effective instrument when struggling with a complex situation, holding too many varied factors to be simultaneously weighed. It clears the mind and places levels of import where they need to be placed. But no man is an emotional data bank and, without intending to sound alarmist, the step of writing a daily inventory places the alcoholic in a position of jeopardy. It moves him *farther* from his fellow man. Strangely, these people who hold so dear the group concept fail to see the futility intrinsic to a routine of *isolated, moral self-instruction.* For example: I may thoughtlessly say something unkind to X. I record this that evening in my journal. As I set it down, I am filled with remorse, and decide to apologize the next day. I do, X is forgiving, and life goes on. But what if I hadn't written down my lapse of manners? Would I have forgotten what I had roughly said a few hours earlier? No. Which I certainly would have, were I the sort of person who hurts others thoughtlessly. The sort of person *who would not have seen that there was an insult to record.*

The diarist of the wrong is also the man reading it and choosing how best to act on it. The two are inextricably linked. How can it be assumed that his response to his recorded action will be more mature than the action itself? It is dangerous to set down any form of behavior with the goal of perusing and amending it in the future, for in writing it down you are *giving substance to what may not be the truth of the situation.* And no one, even with the finest intentions, can catalogue all the qualifying factors which brought forth that behavior at the moment in which it was conducted. How do you record what you don't exactly recall, or perspectives of which you were unaware? What may be seen after the fact as an insult given or received may have been a perfectly legitimate response at the time. Conversely, there is something offensively self-congratulatory in registering your own good deeds. Behavior, even at its most ostensibly simple, is far more complex than any few lines can relate. The workings of a sane mind in a civilized society function with an ever-changing, endlessly multiplying and shifting set of variables. This is as common as common sense can be, and the AA inventory directive always puts me in mind of a fool diving into the back of his computer, moving wires and peering at microchips, to better understand how it works.

I believe without question that emotional affairs and issues are best looked at through logical eyes; are, in fact, better served by it, for logic cannot diminish the power of the emotions themselves. It is no more than a tool. Do I then contradict myself here? No. Because, while elements of the heart and soul may *fall into* familiar regions, categories cannot be superimposed on them. Therein would lie an inversion, a lessening of the value of those priceless components. Which is precisely what the inventory step seeks to accomplish, albeit unwittingly. It is a childish, unrealistic extension of a natural process. I do not believe that a sober human being requires crib notes to walk through life.

Fifteen:

Heroes

I knew a young man who had for a number of years a substance abuse problem. He snorted and smoked several illegal drugs; while he had not yet encountered serious trouble with the law, he had already done considerable damage to his nasal cavities. And everyone, himself included, saw deeper trouble coming fast.

So he checked into an expensive and highly praised rehabilitation center. This place had a reputation for success, success based upon dramatic strategies in addressing the psychological issues underscoring the patient's addiction. The patient's family, in fact, were encouraged to sit in on sessions; feelings could be expressed, old wounds reopened, and understandings hitherto impossible reached. This, at least, was the policy followed with the young man of my acquaintance.

Within days of his admittance the young man made a remarkable turn-around. He was physically cleansed and almost immediately displayed great insights into his past and a solid determination for a better future. Moreover, he became a sort of team leader in whichever group he happened to be in. He was naturally charismatic, but it was the almost heroic leadership qualities he manifested which drew others to him and brought forth educated optimism from the doctors. He was in every sense a stellar example of their treatment.

It was early in his recovery, soon into his stay at the clinic and the change he underwent, that I heard about this wonderful transformation. It is not easy to relate this, for I don't see how I can and still avoid the persona of an evil spirit, or at best an I-told-you-so sort. But the truth is that this news brought out in me one reaction, and one reaction only: the boy is in worse trouble than they know. And this recovery will end with his stay at that place. Of this I was sure. Very little time proved me correct.

All right, then. On what was my certainty based? The young man's history was too brief for me to have merely and snidely been pointing to a trail long established. His problem was also removed from my own, in terms of the substance itself. But I had seen a few examples of such miraculous reversals in AA halls. I had known one or two drinkers who embraced recovery with an enthusiasm to bring cheers from their loved ones. I had seen all of them fall, and rapidly.

Once again human nature must be looked to, and addiction – to liquor, to cocaine, to anything – be placed in its lesser, though still of course momentous, proportion. Too much zeal is never to be trusted, in anything we as people undertake. It isn't so much that it cannot last; rather, the passion itself must be seen as merely symptomatic. For, upon examination, the object of it is usually unimportant to the person so charged up about it. We tend to associate such explosions of short-lived ardor with adolescence. Teens get transfixed, then teens get bored. And I don't think it a coincidence that the same pattern often appears in the addict, or the alcoholic.

I wish the doctors at the clinic I spoke of had shared, or at least entertained, this point of view. They might have spared the young man further turns on the carousel of his addiction. But that is moot. I bring this up, this false heroism of the newly recovered, because it is real, and because a group such as AA feeds it.

Think about it. An AA meeting normally consists of a leader or spokesman, a number of old-timers or regulars, a few nervous, new faces, and a larger amount of people in between: those trying again, those experimenting with it, those in denial, those compelled to sit in by law. A false hero is good for none of these, as he is no good for himself. He sets up an impossible goal to the new, the ones so new that they can't know the courage and determination they see is not real; he often fools the regulars or is welcomed by them, for they cling to such success stories as badly as the novices; and he scares the in-between by virtue of his seemingly easy adjustment. Ironically, it is those in what is called 'denial' who can usually see through the hero's unintentional façade.

It isn't just AA. It isn't perhaps fair of me to single out that organization for permitting, in its thousands of daily meetings, this unfortunate and self-deluded person to hold forth. But these pages take on AA groups, and the fact remains that all groups love heroes. They provide a center, a glowing attraction. And few present, especially in the unsure state of the alcoholic, are able and/or willing to look within the source of the light and question its authenticity.

The intelligent alcoholic, struggling with his disease and his life, must know that to believe in nearly instantaneous recovery is to believe in the circus. Such a thing is intrinsically false, for real addiction envelopes too much to be so quickly thrown off. It blankets every aspect of the drinker's or addict's life; time, much time, must pass before he can even begin to know again what is real and what was manufactured by the drug. And then starts the tedious process of despising what is left, accepting what is left and, finally, being unutterably grateful for what is left. But should you find yourself hearing a hollow victory speech made too soon by someone far too fresh into recovery, do not hate him for it. He will be the one to pay, and the fault isn't even his.

Heroes. While we're on the subject, I'd like to digress into my own experience with the make-believe variety…

There's a bad short story called *The Fate of the Phoenix* yellowing with age among my personal papers. Not altogether bad, I think; it has its moments, as well as an ending too good for the seriously flawed body of it. I wrote it many years ago, struggled with it from time to time, and then filed it with other imperfect projects in a manila envelope labeled 'Needs Work'. It is unfortunate, though perhaps inevitable, that the contents of that envelope have evolved from works-in-progress to something like extremely personal souvenirs.

But the phoenix itself remains a sort of personal icon for me, and was long before I had any reason to take a second look at its traditional symbolism. (The first title for this series of essays, in fact, was THE PHOENIX PROTOCOLS.) My fascination with it is rooted in what may be the only habit I shared with other children: reading comic books. I collected *The Uncanny X-Men*, and they were not merely my favorites; they were the only comic book characters I cared about. They are, for the uninformed, a band of mutants, born with paranormal abilities, "hated and feared by a world they are sworn to protect." Protect from whom, exactly? Other mutants, of course, gifted with less attractive powers and correspondingly baser desires. The conundrum of being despised by the world while perpetually rescuing it; it has no more sophistication or novelty than the tale of the outlaw gunslinger in the old West. I didn't care. My total devotion to these heroes and imaginative identification with them may well have been the most ordinary facets of my childhood.

Children grow up, or they think they do. I joined the ranks of all those other kids who lose interest in the infantile pursuit of comic books. One develops new avocations and fantasies, and it is probably a good and necessary thing that we cannot know then that advancing age does little in the way of turning a fantasy into anything other than what it was from the start. So I stopped buying my *X-Men*, and discarded those I had. (How many other young collectors, I wonder, now regret tossing away those books of their youth? It's a bit disquieting to see the comic you once paid a quarter for fetch a thousand dollars at an auction.)

I don't recall the exact year it all came back to me, but I think it is no coincidence that I returned to my old favorites around the time I began drinking. I was in my early twenties, I know; I think I was happy. I had come to the conclusion that life was quite all right because, no matter what irritations a day or my job held, I could have a few drinks just about any time I liked. I remember the convenience store in my home town. I stopped in for cigarettes one day and my eye was caught by that comic book title from my past, brand-new, on a circular rack. I bought it out of affectionate curiosity, and was shortly dumbfounded by the changes which had taken place in the field. Comic books had become cosmopolitan. Through reading that particular book and others which followed it, I saw a new world. Gone were hideous bad guys and simple-minded plots; *good* guys were unattractive now, and plots had given way to almost Chekhovian musing. There were references to apartment-hunting, relationships and, of all things, addiction. (For the record, Iron Man…well, *resigned* due to alcoholism and, more recently, Captain Britain can be seen pushing aside a glass of the whiskey he had been turning to with alarming frequency. Excelsior, comics industry.) A political aspect was added, as well; mutants were now targets of racism. They were still despised, but no longer quite as feared.

Most astounding of all to me was learning that Jean Grey, *nom de guerre* Marvel Girl, one of the five founding members of the *X-Men* in 1963, had become the phenomenally powerful Phoenix. She then became the even more awesome, but mad, Dark Phoenix. Then she killed herself.

I was fascinated, and had to know more. And I was then, so to speak, off and running. My new attachment to collecting and reading past issues of the *X-Men*, particularly those which narrated Jean's ascent and demise, paralleled the increasing tendency to resort to fantasy and melodrama I was developing. Which, of course, was fueled not only by my drinking, but by the almost thrilling *anticipation* of the drinking I was sure to do. Days off from work became a well-loved, eagerly awaited ritual: I would take the train into New York (my home base was forty minutes away, in New Jersey), and literally run from the subway stop at

Sixth Avenue and West Third Street in the Village to the comic book dealer down the block. His was a seedy little shop; I remember a huge hole in the wall which housed, as improbable as it must sound, a raccoon. But this was still the city, and he always had the latest issues, as well as good prices on the more vintage material. Purchases made, I would run through Washington Square Park, stealing glances at the illustrated panels of the books now and then. Like a child. And this child always had as his final destination for the afternoon a certain bar on Third Avenue.

Now, disguising what was true once for the sake of what I know to be true now may not be a vile thing, but it is dishonest, and can do no good. In those days, I would steel myself before entering the bar. (I had to; I never felt *safe* until that first drink was in front of me. By the third, I was invulnerable.) I would order, take a healthy but unobtrusive sip, light a cigarette, open a comic book, and I was as happy as I can ever recall being. I enjoyed the enormous satisfaction of hurling myself into the reverie of the story, feeling myself enter into it as the liquor entered into me. And I took pleasure in the picture I was sure I presented, if not to the world, then to the bartender and the other patrons: someone young, not unattractive, restrained, and equipped with what had to be perceived as a charming eccentricity. *Was* anyone looking and, if so, was this the effect produced? Maybe, now and then. It didn't matter, because I was sure of it at the time. To have believed otherwise would have been to admit reality into the scene. I was always polite, always controlled, and would leave after six or seven drinks. But reality had no place there.

There were other idiocies in those days, adjuncts to my addiction and its fictive home. They are ridiculous, as much of what I was and did became increasingly ridiculous. Let me then return to the reality of today, and say my last word about heroes.

I said just above that my time in those bars was the happiest I can recall ever spending. That must seem strange, or at least inappropriate; I personally don't know of any recovered drinker who talks with affection of his barroom past. We are pretty much warned against such idling, and not just by AA. A reflex tells us that to see that past as fun or desirable is to set up a return to it.

But here I turn to truth, and not because I am a virtuous person. I turn to it because I am *more afraid* of denying what I know to be true. I fear greater danger from that, no matter the possible short-term benefit of wearing temporal blinders. Since ending my drinking my strength has never abandoned me though, as with everyone, it has its ebbs. My intelligence, or at least the core of it, remains as well. And it allows me to know and accept several contrary things at once. It permits me to go back in my mind and remember a few hours of alcohol-induced confidence and ease, of feeling brave and happy in a bar. It also leaves room for me to know that those days are forever gone, and that a projected return to them is unthinkable, as long as I wish to continue living. That I can retain both knowledges, the memories and the current awareness, hardly makes me a hero. But it contributes to my being a man, as your intelligence and unwillingness to falsify your own past enhances your own humanity. Or will, when you are free.

Sixteen:

Darker Days

When is a spiral not a spiral? When every step turns, how can a turning point be seen? And can anyone be trusted to say for sure, looking back?

I recall a talk show I watched a few years ago. The panel was debating the veracity of what is known as re-birthing therapy. As I understand this procedure, deeply suppressed memories, even those from infancy, are brought to the surface through a recreating of the patient's entry into the world. There were those on this show who had emerged from it, claiming to be whole for the first time in their lives. They could consciously recall *everything* now, and previously crippling social disorders were suddenly explicable.

One doctor took issue with this treatment, and his argument made sense to me. We are not, he pointed out, video playing machines. Each time we delve into our pasts and summon a memory, we *edit* it. It undergoes changes made through the circumstances of the remembering or the telling, changes brought about by the subtle differences in us as we age. He did not deny the enormous usefulness in memory exploration as a psychiatric tool; he simply issued a rather wise warning to accompany it.

I take that warning under heavy consideration now. I've heard too many stories from alcoholics wherein their pasts were, I am sure, magnified. Such people tend to give themselves away in almost cartoon fashion. Bragging, any bragging, has its own easily identifiable scent and body language. (Besides, on a more pedestrian scale, even non-alcoholics love to exaggerate their own Saturday night excesses.) These amplifications from the drinker usually take the peculiar tack of reverse boasting; things, as they relate them, were more horrible, more damning, and all-around worse than the next guy's. They even drank more. This perverse chest-puffing is a cousin to the glorification of self-destruction, and I want to address that in a bit. But I tell myself to be careful as I go into my own worst times. I have a purpose here, and even the relatively minor sin of bravado can only deter it. I never drank shoe polish out of desperation. I never hit anybody with a car, and I never stole from anyone. But I lived for many years with no other aspiration than securing enough liquor to get me through the day. And that can stand, I think, without embellishment. It was quite bad enough.

In the late 1980's I had gotten myself a job as a bartender in New York, at a Wall Street pub. Getting the job was easy enough; I was sent through an agency and taken on for the following day. Of course they hired me. I came across as a relatively attractive, highly experienced applicant. This was an image I could still convey, despite a daily consumption of at least a quart of Scotch. I was still young, regardless of the internal damage I was wreaking, and had the...well, elasticity of youth. (In my early teens, I wrote in a diary that people don't seem to mind moral decay, as long as it isn't physically apparent. I have no idea what prompted me to set that down, so long ago.) So, through the offices of short-lived good impressions and what was left of youthful stamina, I made my commute on the next morning.

The glasses of liquor I had with my coffee got me dressed and to the train station. The hip flask in my pocket was a security measure for the half-hour ride into town. After five minutes on the subway, I would be safe behind a bar. All my bases were covered. They had to be, for I had passed the stage of being sanguine in knowing I could drink *later*. The desire to feel euphoria had quit me some time before, and was never thought of. Maintenance was everything; I would be all right as long as alcohol was within reach.

There was, then, no need to enter the bar I walked by that morning, a dingy bar just around the corner from my new job. The neon lights were on; they were serving at eight in the morning. No need at all to go in. Except that I had time to kill, and this was just too happy a situation to pass by. Why does a miser play with his hoard, anyway? Enter it I did, and I want very much to say that here was my turning point. But it wasn't. Here was where I knew absolutely and consciously that people didn't matter, because strangers in a bar were people too, and drinking would turn them into whatever I wanted them to be. But I knew that before, too.

Part of me expected to be eyed suspiciously by the bartender and by any patrons, upon walking in at such an early hour. They were there of course for the reasons that brought me through the door, but I still anticipated at least a fleeting look of disdain thrown in my direction. What I did *not* expect, and what gratified me in the weeks of visits to come, was the overwhelming sense of *acceptance* I felt. No, I had no wish to be a member of anything, even an entourage so enticingly suicidal, but here was something different: a completely tacit understanding between myself, the man behind the bar, and the others drinking. Those others were not derelicts. They were well-dressed men of business, periodically checking their watches and gauging if the time allowed for another vodka double. There was no conversation in the place. The only phrases to be heard concerned orders and payment, and even these were done so quietly as to be inaudible. *No one spoke.* I felt immeasurably relaxed. I had made it. Amateur standing was behind me. I was in.

That job of mine lasted for about a month. Others followed it, and a litany of these places is pointless. Things became more difficult because I had also pretty much stopped eating, save for the occasional sandwich when absolutely necessary. I had taken to vomiting every morning, and several times in the course of the day, since doing so made me feel…not better, but alive. I moved a few more times, usually remembering to toss out the bottles kept under my bed when I left. My descent was accelerated now; drying-outs become more frequent, and more wretched. The telling of this, incidentally, is not painful. In fact, it's all rather easy. Friends have afterward said that it wasn't *me* behaving this way, but of course it was. It was me addicted. But the passing of time gives me the luxury of feeling that it was someone else cascading down. As, similarly distanced, anyone might recall his own childhood through different eyes.

The last withdrawal I would go through occurred six or seven years ago. (I am honestly not sure. Normally precise in matters of recall, I think I deliberately choose to be careless about that particular date. And why on earth would I wish to commemorate it? May I not be just grateful that it happened?) I was sitting in my parents' condo. They had gone to stay with the rest of the family; I had the place to myself, and thought it a good time for another dry spell to commence. I didn't especially *want* to stop drinking, even then. But certain forces were at play simultaneously. For one thing, I knew I would have to pull myself together if I hoped to get work again, and thus buy liquor again. More, though, an awareness was circling my head, not quite coming through to me. It was there, troubling me like a name you know you know, but can't quite grasp. Although I couldn't distinguish it yet, I had a sense of something ominously large.

I sat in my father's chair, watching an episode of the FAMILY TIES situation comedy. I can hear the dialogue today. It was going to be a sleepless night, I knew, as I monitored myself for signs of trouble. On other such occasions, walking without falling down was impossible for me while withdrawing from alcohol. I sat there, and checked the time. It was twenty minutes past four, in the morning. Fifteen hours, approximately, without a drink. I was handling it, I thought. If I could make it through the next day, perhaps even take some cold water without retching it, I would be through the worst.

Geena Davis, an actress on the show, was suddenly yelling at Michael J. Fox' character, but she was yelling too loudly. The voice seemed to fill the living room. And it was ubiquitous, not confined to the panel on the television set. At that moment, what had eluded me before made itself known to me, and in the most terrifying way imaginable. I cannot properly convey the abject horror which seized me, but I remember *knowing*, as concretely as I have ever known anything, that I was going to die. Then, and there. The force of this certainty paralyzed me. With more courage than I would have believed to be in my possession, I ran to the door. The lock would not turn, and my fumbling desperation only delayed my escape. But escape I did. To hours of walking outside, talking myself through my fear, and waiting for a sun that seemed unwilling to rise.

I have told this story to the few people close to me, and they have reacted in various ways. However, once they accept the sincerity of it as absolute, as not hyperbolized, they tend to speculate on the possibility of God having tapped me on the shoulder. I am a Catholic, a Christian; of course, this has gone through my mind, and more than once. I have come to the conclusion that I cannot know that. I *do* know that I was fortunate. Another may say I was blessed.

I thought long and hard before setting this particular story down. That the evening in question could be interpreted as a mystical or spiritual awakening, that religion would enter into it, ran at cross purposes to what I believe an alcoholic should know. But what happened to me was real. Can I reconcile my faith in an alcoholic's power to free *himself* after relating an incident so open to transcendental rendering?

I can, for the two are, in my mind, one. No dissembling here, or fancy footwork. Personally, I believe something other than myself was in the living room on that night. *That doesn't matter.* Faith, as I have said, is essentially personal, and the God of my faith is uninterested in homage being paid for a service done. He is absolute in my mind, and requires no expression of gratitude beyond that which is in my heart. What I personally believe regarding my experience is unimportant, *to you*. If a message was handed to me from my God, fine. And if an extraordinary chain of chemically-induced activity somehow exploded in my consciousness, fine. For how can I acknowledge anything as being apart from the workings of my God? *The result was the same*, and amazingly mundane. For I was not filled with inspiration from that evening on. Nor was I in any discernible way spiritually different. I simply knew something I had always known from the start, and had shrugged away, years before.

The spiral we began with. So much can be said about each of our spirals, and so many steps on each may be pointed to as the *one*, the deciding moment. Yet they all share the same, rather frightening quality: every move on a spiral is a turning point. Every step is pivotal. Yet if there is one single step to which we as alcoholics can attach the greatest responsibility, it is the first. It is the drink you can't remember. Not the first drink you ever had, but the first taken on the sly, taken earlier than any before. It truly does happen in that moment. We know what we're doing. We elect to abandon reason, aware of the consequences and irrationally choosing to set them aside. In that instant, we betray ourselves. We surrender our minds and commit to a life of excuse-making and rationalizing.

Seventeen:

A Change of Passage

How many alcoholics and drug addicts have written about, commented on, and all-around fell under the spell of the allure of self-destruction? Some, I think, become so immersed in it that they are unaware of its pull and truly believe they are on a dangerous, exciting course alone. In a sense, they are. Others, like myself, can see through the glamour of bringing about one's own destruction, but make pitifully feeble attempts to alter direction. Because that glamour is as strong as any physical addiction, and a powerful element of any addiction's psychological pull. It satisfies so many desires, and is actually made more formidable *through*, and not in spite of, daily life.

The person on this path sets himself apart, for he courts what everyone seeks to avoid: the end. This perversity is even attractive to other, sane people, *as long as appearances are kept up*. While that happy state continues, devil-may-care conduct reaches its zenith of fascination. Anyone can waste money. Who can match the wild extravagance of tossing aside time, and life? All of which comprises the only praise I am prepared to shower on such a person. I was there. It is all false, and degrading.

However. *Can* the seduction of self-destruction be successfully combated on paper? I am sorely tempted to use a familiar approach, to affirm that a world of possibilities exists for the drinker who turns his back on that lure; that there are, moreover, large and small emotional riches of which he has yet to conceive. But I can no more instill in him a guarantee of potential, hitherto unrevealed feeling than I can truthfully say I share his own, individual anguish. I have one recourse: I can carry on with my faith in the science of emotion, and appeal to my reader's mind.

If you: anticipate *with pleasure* your assured routine of spending several hours a day in a bar; if you feel most *at ease* when your first drink is set before you; if the second or third lends *confidence* to you; and if any one of these minor activities gives you a sense of being *at peace, convivial, contemplative, or invincible*, then it cannot be disputed that you possess a wealth of sensations which you yourself find interesting, and which makes the world around you interesting.

Well and good. Only one dilemma presents itself. You are inducing these feelings and sensations chemically, via a substance which damages every cell in your body. It is always degenerative and, whatever the rate of erosion, will eventually consume even your most primitive bodily functions. As there is no strict dichotomy between the body and the mind, each will suffer in varying degrees, and at different times. But the collapse will come. If I were to personify this breakdown, I would say that it can afford to be generous and herald its final arrival with lesser episodes.

The mistake you have made is that made by all addicts. You have confused *one source* for all of the affections and disinclinations we possess and exercise which make living a desirable state of affairs. You have, so to speak, taken the road for the destination. This is understandable. Alcohol initially enhances how we digest an experience. It is later in our addictions that we employ it as the experience itself. And, so addicted, our minds let our cravings do the navigating for us. Again, perfectly understandable. But a blunder, and a spectacular one, it is.

Removing that counterfeit path, that source, from your life is relatively easy. Living without it is not, not for quite a while. You must have faith. Not religious faith, but the faith you hold in knowledge, in knowing a tree for a tree, a stone for a stone. You must maintain an unshakable conviction in the *reality* of knowledge. *You know* what you are capable of feeling. You have felt a great deal, under the influence. But influence, any influence, is *no more* than that. There are avenues to what you need, avenues which will not harm you and which avail themselves to you only when you are free. There is no point in my promising you experiences you'll be sure to have when sober. They are the sensations and impressions you have now. They aren't going anywhere. But I would like to paraphrase Edward Albee and tell you that sometimes you have to go a long way *out* of your way, in order to come back a short distance correctly.

Eighteen:

Pride, and Prejudice

It has occurred to me that these pages may be misconstrued. Of course it has. If they are read at all, they will be read by people with a decided interest in alcoholism: their own, or another's. Alcoholics Anonymous has become a byword in our land for recovery. This is so pervasive as to make any other path seem farfetched, and specious. Thus, a hundred additional declarations affirming the good I believe AA has done in the world will be ignored by those seeing only my criticisms of that eminent body.

But that doesn't preoccupy me a great deal. Such people will also conveniently overlook the near demand I have made for a certain kind of reader, a kind emphatically unlike themselves. Besides, suspicion and criticism are bound to follow anyone who challenges the precepts of a powerful group. (What I fear, in fact, is missing out on valid criticism, the kind that may get lost in a morass of insecure, xenophobic drivel.)

Yet, AA may be a Goliath, but I am an uncomfortable sort of David, and it must be remembered that even an evil-minded David would create just as much division as the virtuous one we all know. It's the numbers that are inescapable here, and the sizes of the contestants; little against big, unknown against famous—always a formula for splitting camps. But I cannot concern myself with that, either. All I can care about is speaking to the people who will listen to me in the first place, those who were uncomfortable in Goliath's pockets to begin with. There is no message without that particular audience.

We live, however, in the world. Even you and I, reader. One thing more needs saying before I take your arm and lead you aside for the last time.

I have just said, and meant, that I will not bother with uncalled-for reactions to my thinking. Nor should you, whether your own ideas mirror mine or not. But be prepared for them, accept them, and relegate to them the sideline status they deserve. For one thing, accusations of elitism will come your way. This will constitute a somewhat fractional part of the trials you will undergo, but a galling one it is, and you will face it. I already have, whatever the fate of this book.

Such an assessment of my character was indirectly thrown my way when I naively tried to connect with other alcoholics at AA meetings; when I tried to impart my feelings of uneasiness about the organization. Approaching the most seemingly sympathetic souls I could find with this anxiety, I was invariably warned that I would fail on my own. Whatever was holding me back must be cast aside. I must abandon my pride and embrace the collective. And I had as well an uncomfortable perception of being regarded as a snob. As someone who thought himself too good for the likes of AA.

I am. So are you. Just as a contented member of Alcoholics Anonymous is, in his own way, too good to spend time with me. I am not just playing with words here: if you have ever been considered an elitist, and you are an intelligent person, you give this serious consideration. I did, and in short order was rewarded with an almost righteous wrath directed at those who would level such a charge. For AA halls are practically bursting with arrogance. The people inside are, from my experience, supercilious in their attitudes, in their smugness, and, above all, *in their numbers.*

We live in a country where the extravagant show of wealth or education is thought to be vulgar. Thus, the masses themselves have acquired the position of dictating what is and what is not acceptable. We have, seemingly, no class system. Money and power remain synonymous, of course, but this is not to be acknowledged. The time of the *vertical* caste system is gone. Fine. Its destruction was one of the motivating forces in the founding of our country. But the people, in one form or another, set the standard. So we now have a class structure numerically based. Politicians appeal to the common man, and advertisers covet, not a discriminating few, but the largest market share. Whoever can assert his affiliation with *the people* has a sense of privilege, of pronouncing judgment in all things, once reserved for persons of rank. The masses, therefore, hold the *social* veto in their hands as well as the political variety. And they use it no more wisely than did their aristocratic ancestors.

I've sat in meetings filled with that diversity of humanity of which AA is so proud. Would that their populist and elitist air were limited to their philosophies. But because they are so many, they command other discretions as well. As a group, they hold prerogatives which will not permit entry of an idea, not because it is antithetical to their thinking, but because it is presented incorrectly. In other words, I have been disregarded because I spoke well. I was *understood*, mind you; I do know that luxuriant language is worthless if meaning is lost. But I also know with certainty that I was mistrusted. I was not speaking the language of the common man. (This was, incidentally, confirmed to me by a well-intentioned man who had actually listened to what I said. He had heard a few disparaging remarks about my words by the coffee machine, and was genuinely trying to help me better fit in, for meetings to come. Elitist? If I am an elitist, I am a toothless beast, indeed.)

From there, I believe it was generally presupposed by the crowd that I felt I had *nothing* in common with the others. Not even alcoholism. At least, from their point of view. I do not exaggerate. People, and not only condescendingly blue-collar alcoholics, seem to enjoy leaping over logic, from one fact to a preposterous conclusion. I felt misplaced at AA; I did not believe I had much, if anything, in common with its members; ergo, I must not believe myself to be an alcoholic.

I knew I was an alcoholic many years before my addiction crippled my life. But what was there for me to justify, and to whom? Anything at all of which would have fallen on the wrong ears. And why travel in this tortuous loop? I had had quite enough of circuitous journeying, courtesy of my drinking. Should you, reader, confront this confused interpretation of your solo course, leave it be. It will frustrate you, but let it do nothing else to your state of mind. AA members would agree with me when I say that you are powerless to change the thinking around you. They would also, as we know, extend this helplessness into the arena of your own abilities. But we have already saluted, and walked away.

There will be another source of angst waiting for you, and it is harder to dismiss. People still close to you, family members and old friends, will be as uncomprehending as the strangers you turned from. They will be distressed that you do not attend meetings. They will take this unwillingness to participate in the program as proof of your insincerity, and await with an understandable mixture of vindication and sadness the day you next stumble to their door. Do not try to persuade them otherwise, because you cannot. Realize from the start that they have good reason for thinking as they do; every reason, in fact, and that's *without* taking into account your own history of addiction. AA members fall, and they're with *the program*; how can you not?

The greater degree of intimacy you share with them will go nowhere in breaking down barriers. Not where your recovery is concerned. All it will do, in fact, is cause you the greater grief at being so doubted. *Do not take this mistrust personally*. Do not take it at all. Just as in the vortex of your habit everyone is reduced to the status of an outsider, so, too, must that be the case in the first throes of your recovery. The dearest people to you were, consciously or not, there while you were drowning. There was nothing they could do, but they were there. You were content then to let them remain apart from you. Let them wait a little while longer, as you return to life.

Nineteen:

The Last Verse

Nothing I've said, and no way of thinking I've adopted and recommend, was born out of ease. This should come as no surprise, even to the non-drinker. Quitting alcohol is miserable, and hard. Staying off of it is harder, at least for a while. The entire affair, in a crowd or alone, is a vile one. I tell you to *embrace that from the start*; to grit your teeth, as it were, and go in as if you were fighting for your life. As you are, or will be.

But—and this is vital—do not expect to awake on the first day you are physically all right again and find a more beautiful world. That underlined AA's agenda to me, with the addendum that I would continually have to prove myself fit for this grand, exciting existence by remaining clean. And with my sincere conviction that alcoholics who are at home and sober in AA remain with it reinforced once again, I take off my gloves for the last time.

AA seems to subscribe to the notion that life holds endless rewards and challenges, all available to the sober man, all waiting for him outside the door of the meeting room he will everlastingly visit. They love best the stories from their most ebullient members, stories born from the thrilling aspects of life they had previously been unable to see. Tales relating the deep, satisfying happiness found in resumed, ordinary activities are even more welcome. Work the steps, they say. Attend meetings, find a sponsor, and it will all come to you. *As long as you are strong enough for it.*

I do not believe this, and neither should you. Oh, life is, I believe, a glorious thing. People, on the other hand, are draining, demanding, and, more often than not, an obstruction to finding the good things in life. Why else would we gather only a few to us in the courses of our lives, to hold the multitudes at bay? Why, especially, are you and I not content to stay clean and enjoy all the new friendships AA has to offer?

Would that AA's outlook were more rooted in truth. But it isn't, you know. It would be far easier to take a blow, such as the misery of withdrawal, and have it done with than to confront, daily, a world with no excitement in it at all. AA, however, cannot acknowledge this. And it is in this repudiation that much of their flawed theory lies. If the impetus for remaining sober is the rich existence they foresee for the newly sober man, then alcohol itself must take on mythic proportions. Surely no mere chemical could be so compelling that it draws one back to it, even from rediscovered, splendid life? Furthermore, how staggeringly potent is this substance, that continued immersion in the club-like environment of AA is necessary to avert it, *in addition* to, again, the full life the recovered person is currently enjoying? That is no drug. That is a deity.

Alcoholics Anonymous does not deal well with people like us, people who do not fit in with programs. I understand the gap between us; I have, in a sense, created it in turning my back to them. All other differences aside, I never once thought of liquor as anything more than *what it is*, even in my worst times. This is a point of view they do not consider. It is at odds with the superhuman stature they accord alcohol. But far more evasive is their blindness to a basic situation within their walls: all the alcoholics who enter the program, and fall out again. And enter, and fall. Many really try very hard to work the steps, to absorb the thinking. They want it to be the last treatment they will need. How can such resolve, then, go wrong?

AA exalts alcohol ,and gives it whatever power you yourself may have refrained from endowing it with, because they themselves have misgivings about that life you will be returning to. It is their psychological back-up plan. You drink too much, and join AA; you stop drinking and then find the world unendurably mundane without it; and you would return to drinking. Except that it isn't just plain old liquor you are craving. You are told that it is frighteningly powerful. You are told that the sheer, satanic *might* of liquor is what is luring you in. It isn't, it cannot be, that life without a control substance is too dull.

Well, it is. It is a combination of work and leisure, and much of that leisure is filled with unsuccessful attempts to find pleasure. Or the initially gratifying outlet of a relationship and/or beginning a family is seized, which in due course carries with it innumerable duties and obligations. I must pause, reader: understand that I believe life is an indisputably excellent thing, and more than worth every chore it demands of you. But only a child looks for joy as a *right*. Living is under no obligation to make itself endearing to us. We are, in fact, obliged to seek out those facets of it which, ideally, both please us and enhance us as human beings. This is as good as it gets. Personally, I think it is magnificent. But it is rarely thrilling. Nor is it easy, and by no reckoning can that which is wonderful about it be had quickly. No matter how urgent your need.

I mentioned earlier that the intelligent alcoholic has only one lesson to learn. I address him directly now, for he is the only reader I set out to reach. If you continue to drink because drinking is indispensable to you, you will eventually die from it. You will have collapsed in many other ways before this happens, and the entire ordeal, from whatever point you are currently at, will become increasingly messy and painful. The simplicity of this truth makes it no easier to know, but there is no way around it.

If you choose to go on with your addiction, it is incumbent upon you to accept everything that choice entails. That is, make the last decision as a man or woman it will ever be in your power to make, and leave your life. Absent yourself from your family, your friends, your work. It is all crumbling anyway. This is the only remotely honorable thing you can do, under the circumstances. Whatever your opinion of the people and circumstances of your surroundings, no matter how dismissive you are of all of it in the midst of your addiction, *you do not have the right to drain everything around you.* In taking this road, you call on a courage perhaps more formidable than that you would require for salvation. This is not, happily, an irony with which you will long need concern yourself.

But you have read this far. Far enough, I hope, to know that there is another way to go.

There is no language available to me which will make my message new. We both know that. Yet the world has persistently operated on the same premises, and run on the same tracks, since it began. It has done so, not because of original insight delivered, time and again, to waiting civilizations, but because each message is new *as it is taken in by one person.* A thought, an idea, lives for the first time when it is incorporated into the mind and spirit of a man or woman. Love, and every possible expression of it, should have been exhausted as a source of interest by the advent of the first recorded decade. It certainly has been run dry to *us.* Until, of course, an attraction explodes in our lives. No, I don't handle here quite so elegant a subject. Love, indeed. No; I merely traffic in the business of life.

It means absolutely nothing that a program which works for millions fails for you. The only consequence of this is that you must rely on yourself, a circumstance which may be impeded by a support group as easily as it may be enhanced by one. A circumstance, incidentally, every member of any support group finds himself in when the meeting is over and the lights are out. Camaraderie, specifically the fellowship of a program, is self-perpetuating because *it has to be.* And you are just as likely to be misled by one individual's strategy of recovery as you are to be inspired by another's.

Do not expect a sublime and fulfilling life upon drying out. You have as much reason to anticipate such an existence's coming your way as the man who never touched a drink in his life. Your life will most likely be, for quite some time after you achieve sobriety, no better than when you first started chipping away at it. You will probably carry with you, for an equally long time, vulnerability and resentment. The non-alcoholic is ignorant of those weights. This will feel grossly unfair. Perhaps it is. But it is the way things are.

Turn to your religious faith only if that is what has *always* been essential to you. The woods, I fear, are full of people who discover God when everything else has been appealed to, when they have nothing else nearby to importune. Have none of it. There will be times in your life, pivotal or trivial, when surrender is the only choice to make; a surrender to your God, or to whatever forces you believe shape the events you cannot face. *This is not one of them.* This is your fight. The stronger your belief in your God, in fact, the *less need* you have to surrender. Maintain your faith, or find it again after recovery, but do not cheapen it.

Do not lose sight of the other faith, of what you *know of this world*. With your own strength will come the inexpressible advantage of suiting yourself, with everything that phrase implies. It will be in your power again to do fine things or conduct yourself badly, and the good you do will have permanence and the blunders you make will not be so bad. You will be free to move in directions you had forgotten. You will know this freedom more fully, too, than one who has never lost it. Nothing will be freely *given* to you, but nothing ever was.

It is stupid and not at all helpful to consider alcohol 'cunning'. It is a chemical substance, a drug. It has no cunning, and it has no power. Those properties belong to you.

Most importantly, I tell you to use your mind. Reason and intelligence are extraordinary things, possessed of great vitality. They are not cold, lifeless assets; they are as integral to the flow of life as the emotions. Use every pathway you know or can find within you to remain clean. Uncover those you were unaware of, and use them as well. See yourself as a hero in a comic book if you like, know that to be ridiculous, and go on with it. Write a journal, not an inventory, and write nothing but expressions of the tedium and anger you will surely experience. Have nothing to do with slogans, because that is all they are, and nobody lives one day at a time. You are striving for something more lasting.

Finally, grant me one, somewhat melodramatic illustration. You may recall the ghost of Jacob Marley's visiting his extant partner, Scrooge, in Dickens' CHRISTMAS CAROL. I come from a similar place, and carry a chain equally ponderous in weight and length. I imagine it is much like your own. But I have written this not to prepare you for spiritual guests, but to draw your attention to something awaiting you; something so easily taken for granted and so quickly lost; something much more tangible than any spectre, but just as phenomenal: *choices.*